BRIAN BERRY

CRITICISM
BITES

dealing with, responding to, and learning from your critics

YouthMinistry.com/TOGETHER

Criticism Bites
Dealing With, Responding to, and Learning From Your Critics

© 2013 Brian Berry

group.com
simplyyouthministry.com

Credits
Author: Brian Berry
Executive Developer: Nadim Najm
Chief Creative Officer: Joani Schultz
Editor: Rob Cunningham
Cover Art and Production: Veronica Preston

ISBN 978-0-7644-7555-9

10 9 8 7 6 5 4 3 2 1   20 19 18 17 16 15 14 13

Printed in the U.S.A.

DEDICATION

I dedicate this book to my friends and colleagues in ministry who daily work to love on students and families with one hand and respond to criticism and unhappy people with the other. You are phenomenal pastors who wrestle with discouragement as a casualty of your love.

To those of you who have a nagging voice in your head that never goes away and says that you should quit, that you're inadequate, or that your shortcomings are your only legacy, this book is for you. Read it carefully. I will humbly remind you, as I remind myself, that voice is not God's. I could specifically name some of you for whom this is your daily struggle, but that would be borderline cruel. So I'm just gonna encourage you to write your name in this blank if that's you. *Hi, my name is _____, and criticism has a way of destroying and discouraging me deeply.*

From the core of my being, I want to say that your life and ministry matter, and this book is for all of us.

To the mentors who have gently, and even at times firmly, corrected my life along the way, this book is in tribute of you. To name a few, I owe my wife Shannon, my mom and dad, Mark Teyler, Mark Wold, Ron Ritchie, Ed Noble, Mark Oestreicher, Tic Long, Scott Berglin, Gino Cunningham, Danny Bowers, and Mark Campbell a debt of gratitude. I am who I am today because you loved me enough to correct me along the way.

TABLE OF CONTENTS

FOREWORD

I don't think I have ever heard anyone say, "I love to be criticized," "Criticism is so awesome," or "Criticism is fuel for my soul!" Nope, I have never heard that because most of the time criticism hurts. It more than hurts, it bites! It can suck the life right out of us and cause us to want to quit whatever it is we are doing. But check this out: If you are in ministry or a leader of any kind, it is inevitable—and if you are in youth ministry it's close to being a constant companion. So you see, we don't have an option but to learn how to deal with it.

Brian states early in the book, *"Your capacity to respond to criticism in ways that honor God is not an optional skill; it is a mandatory tool for all leaders."*

He is 100 percent correct, but oh, if only it was as easy as that sounds. "Cool, I just need to add a new tool to my ministry tool belt and I am good to go."

Dealing with criticism is one of the most difficult challenges in life and yet one of the least adequately addressed.

Most of us are more than aware of our typical, unhelpful responses to being criticized such as ignoring, getting angry, attacking, pouting, justifying, and daydreaming of elaborate ways of getting revenge that will strike a blow but won't end up getting us in jail. We KNOW they get us nowhere, but we go there time and again.

Criticism is so multilayered. It's personal, it's professional, it's called for, it's uncalled for. We see it coming, we are blindsided by it. It is well-reasoned, ill-reasoned, and just flat-out wrong. It comes from both friend and foe. It hits our self-worth, our sense of calling, and our competence.

No wonder it can cut us to the quick and put us into a deep pit of despair. It is nothing to trifle with or attempt to face with simplistic responses.

Fortunately, Brian spares us the simplistic responses and provides four really helpful things.

1. He explores with insight why criticism can be so devastating to us. What is it about being criticized that can so quickly rob us of our joy, confidence, and self-worth? He gets inside us.

2. He provides a path, a way of being, a sense of understanding, a life strategy—whatever you want to call it—along with practical tools to not only survive criticism and to pick your way through its minefield, but to reach a place where you are not just better equipped to survive but actually grow from it in both your personal life and ministry.

3. He puts us on the spot. Brian provides questions for us to have to work through about ourselves. This is not an academic exercise but an opportunity for maturing. We are being discipled in an area of our life we can't ignore. Brian calls us to look in the mirror.

4. He offers truth, real-life situations, and authenticity. This is a nonsense-free zone where Brian helps us face real issues in real life.

I have known Brian for years, and I have criticized Brian. I know that he lives the stuff he is writing about. I know the wisdom found in these pages can be life-giving. Those of you who are youth workers are called to be criticized; you can't avoid it. You must always take risk, take chances, try new things. You will make mistakes (and you should!). You are herding cats, but you are also changing a generation.

Change…risk…new…mistakes…teenagers…parents…pastors…
church janitors…your world invites criticism, and you must learn how to
invite it in as a friend and not run from it as an enemy. Brian will help
you to do that. He knows your world. He is your friend.

Tic Long
With his 34 years of experience in training, equipping, and caring for youth workers
at Youth Specialties, and his heart for youth workers everywhere, Tic is somewhat of a
Yoda to the youth ministry community. He also currently serves as executive pastor at
Journey Community Church in La Mesa, California.

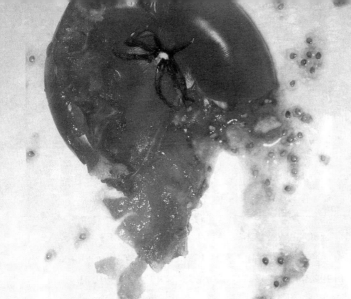

INTRODUCTION

When I started my first full-time job as a youth pastor, I had an unquenchable enthusiasm to make a difference—plus a laptop computer, a shelf of commentaries, and a single-file drawer. My office fit in the trunk of my '65 Mustang, and like that car, I was ready to change the world at Mach speeds. While my youth pastor experience fit on a single sheet of paper, my dreams couldn't fit in the building. So what I lacked in wisdom, I simply made up for in zeal.

In an attempt to increase my wisdom and decrease my zealous cover-ups as a leader, I started going to seminars and leadership training events for pastors and communicators, including several events featuring author, pastor, and leadership guru John Maxwell. One common theme that I heard him talk about was how he did his research to prepare for his books and sermons. To put it simply, John had files. As he went about his daily life, he would cut and clip articles from magazines, newspapers, advertisements—pretty much anything he came across. Once a file got to a certain thickness, then he would write a book or talk.

I loved this idea, and because it was LONG before the days of the Internet, Evernote®, and the digital camera, I joined Maxwell in compiling my own extensive set of old-school hanging file folders. In them, I stored countless illustrative ideas, facts, articles, and even some books I cut up on a variety of subjects. Working with teenagers, I obviously had multiple categories under sexuality and dating, and I had topical folders on everything from addictions to zeal.

I had some odd interests that produced their own files for illustrations. This resulted in a file for the Olympics, one for the Navy SEALs, and one dedicated to people's strange addictions, such as a kid who collected trash or a man who set the world record for popping popcorn. You name it, I probably had a file on it. Before "Google®" was a company or a verb, my co-workers and high school students who were writing papers for school would "Brian search" a word and ask me for a file on some topic. I was vigilant at it, never throwing a magazine away until I had skimmed and gleaned from it. My nemesis was the "to-file pile" that was a bin of stuff I had skimmed and tagged but had no time to file.

But in the beginning, there was one file I didn't have and never had anyone ask me for. It was one I eventually labeled "Criticism," and despite the low demand, it grew quite large—both with some criticism I received and articles I began to devour. It wasn't that I had never received any criticism by the time I started ministry; it was just that I had no idea that managing it would be such a mission-critical part of my job.

Initially, I thought youth ministry was a phenomenal calling. I loved the influence my own youth pastor had on me in high school, and I couldn't wait to put down my part-time summer construction hammer and graduate from college so I could get started. On the construction site I knew I needed gloves, safety glasses, steel-toed shoes, and occasionally a hard hat to keep the inevitable dropped tool or flying wood chip from sending me to the emergency room. But I had no idea that I needed a similar set of pastoral equipment to keep me from heading to the ministry triage wing. It didn't take long before I discovered that youth ministry would involve a constant struggle between two extremes: Side 1—Please God and love on people vs. Side 2—Please people and love on God. I also quickly discovered that keeping Side 1 in the No. 1 slot is easier said than done. A LOT easier said than done.

I once heard a teaching by Andy Stanley at Willow Creek's Global Leadership Summit in which he said, "Leaders have to know when something is a problem to solve and when it is actually a tension to manage."[1] The issue of criticism is not something you solve. It's something you manage. You will always have your critics. I will always have mine. The irony is that even in writing a book on criticism, this, too, will have its critics and, before it is published, will go through a series of critical reviews. Thus, as long as you and I are breathing, the ability to navigate, respond to, and even learn from our critics is a mandatory life skill. This book is not an attempt to solve the issue of criticism or even to get you to a place where you receive it less. The truth is, we cannot control what others criticize anyway. Instead, this book is designed to help us learn to think through and respond to our critics in healthy ways.

So if you've ever let your zeal outrun your wisdom…if you've ever wanted to quit a leadership role…if you've ever cried or lashed out in anger at the cutting remarks from someone who ripped into you for some mistake you made or just some unhappy bystander who "flipped you the bird"…if you've ever received a critical email that you read way too many times… if you've ever found yourself in a cycle of depression that sent you into your own personal dark night of the soul…if you've ever thought, "Is this really worth it?" then we share a kindred spirit. Criticism bites, and this book is for both of us.

To this end, I will make you a promise: As we travel this road together, I will not use "poetic license" to fabricate or make up stories. At times I will change names for my own integrity and to keep this book honest without being accusatory. This is simply the stuff I've bled, discovered, learned, and stumbled into as a husband, dad, and youth pastor.

In the pages that follow, we will examine why criticism hurts so much. We will look at our own hearts, consider why criticism cuts so deeply, and develop some processes by which we can respond to those who are not happy with us. We'll strive to discern when those critical words are truth from God that we should heed and when they are cuts from the enemy that we should flat out ignore. We will seek to examine, wrestle with, and respond to our critics with the same grace and truth that we hope others will give to us.

If that sounds like something you need, then welcome to the painful and necessary journey of doing life and leadership when criticism bites.

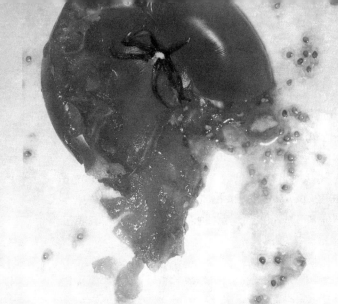

CHAPTER 1
THE DAY
I QUIT

The seed of this book was planted in my life on Thursday, June 25, 1998. It was my fourth wedding anniversary, but oddly enough, it had nothing to do with my marriage. Our anniversary celebration was delayed due to the fact that it was the last night of a weeklong summer camp with our high school ministry at some conference grounds in Northern California—not exactly a romantic escape. I was running the camp with a friend of mine for our youth groups and several other churches. Shannon was there for moral support, while primarily being mom to our 11-month-old son, T.J.

To truly understand this day, you need to know that a couple of years earlier, we had a HUGE water fight on the last night of this very camp. It was epic. Seriously, I know that word is overused, but it was everything *epic* is meant to describe. Picture an infamous experience that no one who was there has ever forgotten. Epic.

Here's how it went down. The youth pastors had been taunted daily by a cabin of senior guys—with notes and hints and full-on harassment—into having a final-night water fight. Since we had no time to really deal with this and no interest in filling hundreds of water balloons at 2 a.m. ourselves, we decided to thwart their plan and raid their cabins of stuff they could attack us with. So on Thursday morning, while everyone was supposed to be in chapel, we raided "Birdland" where they were staying and grabbed trashcan after trashcan of water balloons that they had stashed away in the days before. (I know, great example we were setting. Now wipe that judgment off your face and don't act like you haven't got one of these stories. Ha!) Anyway, we figured we now had so many water balloons that we were sure we had them severely outgunned. There's no way they could refill that many water balloons again with only one afternoon of free time to make it happen.

Wrong. I told you: It was epic.

Later that night we loaded up the back of my full-size truck with six youth pastors, Stream Machine™ water guns, 50-gallon trashcans of water, and a literal truckload of all the water balloons we had stolen from them. The road into their camp was in the center of a ravine, and all the cabins were built on stilts on both sides of the ravine. Without warning, around 11 p.m., we drove my truck up this valley road for our surprise attack as I screamed, "You're going down, suckas!" into the PA system I had installed on my truck, and we began our assault. But by about the time my mouth uttered the second syllable of "suckas," the world began raining water balloons. Seriously—raining! Not only were the campers NOT in their beds or having cabin time, I think the guys from every cabin in the area knew we were coming and were in the bushes, on the roofs, in trees—pretty much everywhere, with thousands of water balloons within reach. I'm convinced some kid went to camp with just the clothes on his back, maybe a change of underwear, and an entire suitcase filled with empty water balloons!

We would never admit it then or in the years that followed, but the truth is, we got destroyed. All the youth pastors blamed me and said I didn't drive far enough up the hill. But in my defense, I stopped because of the inability to see through the wall of balloons coming down on my windshield. I think the military got the "shock and awe" bomb concept from these students. It was so epic that my windshield was literally shattered by a water balloon the size of a basketball that made a direct hit off a cabin roof. It was crazy!

Well, as you can imagine, a water fight like this was the talk of the camp the next morning. In fact, it was all people talked about heading into the next several years of camp. But by 1998, it was a "tradition" we were trying to avoid. The first year was literally unrepeatable, and every year after felt less "epic" and more like "work." Through the years, the girls all wanted to join in, and it morphed from youth pastor vs. students into guys vs. girls. Along the way, a variety of things had been broken in cabins, and there was even water damage we had to pay for. The last night of spiritual experiences was being commandeered by water-fight anticipation. The truth is that the youth pastors really wanted it to go away, but it had become like an unwritten expectation in the camp brochure that was still convincing some students to come to our camp in the first place.

Now, back to June 25, 1998. After dinner on that night, I gathered my counselors to discuss what I thought was a solid compromise. I said something like this: "In order to not spoil the fun and in an attempt to not have an epic water fight near a cabin where I will inevitably have to pay for water damage, here's my new plan. At exactly midnight, all the girls will leave their cabin area to 'secretly' head up to ambush the guys. The guys will do the same, leaving their area to go ambush the girls on a pre-chosen route. As long as we all leave at the right time and take the specified route, they will inevitably 'accidentally' run into one another in the parking lot and have a water fight there. Everyone will get to have their fun, they'll be surprised, and it will be in a safer location."

Everyone thought this was a good idea and agreed to go along—everyone except one of my key volunteers, if not my most key volunteer at the time. I'll call him "John." We were friends. But he was 15 years older than I was, very passionate about his convictions, and in this case it turns out that he was very upset by what I had asked him to do. In his view, I had asked him to lie to his students, something he vowed never to do based on biblical conviction and passion for integrity. In my view, I had asked him to do something akin to not telling them about a surprise party. It was a water fight. But we were at an impasse, and in his mind, it was on the level of asking him to compromise his character. John said, "I don't lie to my small group of guys, and I won't lie to them now." Later he told his cabin group that I had asked him to lie to them, and that night, the history of the water fight died in a firestorm of anger and confusion.

By the time the next morning rolled around, John refused to speak to me. He was going around to the other youth pastors and asking them to correct me in my sin as one of their peers. He was beyond upset, and the 125 or so students I had brought with me were on the fast track toward massive division. I know it sounds trivial and overdramatic, but the whole thing had me in a spiritual, emotional, and mental tailspin. I cried. I yelled at God. I was numb. I could not believe this was happening and had no idea where to turn. It was all I could do to load the buses, get everyone home, and try to keep from losing it in front of my students, who could clearly see that something was not right and knew that it was something between the two people with the most "power and influence" in our youth group.

(SIDE NOTE: If this whole response feels a bit overstated and out of the blue to you, then you understand how I felt—but you're also missing one more piece of backstory. While John and I were good friends, our friendship had been tested by fire before. We shared a passion for Jesus and were both big-voice personalities, but beyond that, our cultural experiences and convictions varied quite a bit. He and I'd had run-ins before over how we did ministry, what we should say to students, and even the role my wife should or shouldn't play in ministry. One such run-in had occurred just a few months before this camp on a Mexico mission trip when John had a disagreement with a student, who in turn cussed at him during their angry altercation. As a result, John threatened to leave our group in Mexico if I didn't do something about it. He said he was prepared to take his wife and go home on the moral grounds of never allowing a teenager to show disrespect for an elder. This felt like a form of blackmail, threatening to leave me stranded with students in a foreign country if I didn't side with him. When we returned to the U.S., we had meetings and mediation with our senior pastor for months to bring restoration to our relationship and to John's relationship with the student in question. It felt like we were just getting to the point where this thing was beginning to heal by the time summer camp rolled around. But clearly, it was still bleeding below the surface, and now the wound was gushing from a pulmonary artery of my soul.)

With all that in mind, when I got home I wanted to crawl into a hole and die (or at least hide for a few months), but I couldn't. My senior pastor was on vacation, and I was set to preach in less than 48 hours. I had a message to finalize, and I had to get my head straight before I stood up in front of the entire church. So Saturday morning I dragged myself to my office and sat down at my desk. I don't even remember what I taught on that Sunday, but I do know what happened in my office that day. As I sat there with my mind and soul spinning, I looked down and saw a book that I had purchased some months before sitting on my desk: *Leaders on Leadership*, which was edited by legendary researcher George Barna. Out of confusion or reflex or divine inspiration, I picked it up and looked at the table of contents. I saw a chapter by H.B. London Jr. titled "Being a Tough but Tender Leader" and decided to give it a read. As I did, the tears began to flow, and I was pretty sure he had written it for one person on the planet: me. I remember literally thinking God was speaking to me through this book as I read a quote inside from Stuart Briscoe that said, "To be a successful pastor one must have the mind of a scholar, the heart of a child, and the hide of a rhinoceros."[2] In that moment I knew two things: (1) I did not have the hide of a rhinoceros, and (2) if that was what it meant to be a pastor, I had a long way to go—and I wasn't sure I even wanted to get there.

The next day I preached my sermon in a trance or something, and then Shannon and I dropped off our son at her parents' house and headed for a three-day getaway we arranged months earlier to celebrate our anniversary. But we both knew this year would now be less about celebration and more about a marital soul searching. I was deeply wounded and desperately needed to rest in the love of my wife and my God. Before I left, I called my senior pastor and left a voice mail on his office line and told him this: "John and I had another massive problem at the end of camp. I'm sure you'll hear all about it. I'm leaving with my wife to celebrate our marriage, think, and pray. I'll be back on Wednesday, and all I ask is that you meet with me before you meet with him."

Over the next three days, my wife and I wrestled with the situation, prayed, and cried. In the end, we concluded that I had somehow signed up for the wrong job. I felt like Jeremiah when he got angry with God and said, *"You deceived me" (Jeremiah 20:7)*. I felt deceived by my Creator and misled by what it meant to be a pastor. This criticism thing was literally more than I could bear. I couldn't do this—and besides, the volunteer I was at odds with was so influential in our youth group and church that I was pretty positive I would cause a church split if I didn't just leave. I decided I needed to quit—but not just quit being a youth pastor at this church. I needed to quit ministry and be something other than a pastor. Like Peter, who in his own funk of confusion went back to fishing after Jesus' death, I thought maybe it was time to pick up the hammer again.

So without going home or getting our son, we checked out from our bed-and-breakfast and drove straight to the church office for a closed-door meeting with my senior pastor. Through tears and deep regret, I said, "I'm sorry, but I don't think I can do this anymore. I think I need to resign."

But much to my surprise, our pastor wouldn't let me. He said he was going to get involved. I told him he couldn't step between John and me in this way and that this was a church-splitting bullet he didn't have to bite. I honestly expected it to cost us both our jobs if he did. He, however, disagreed, and I agreed to humbly submit and follow his lead.

In my despair, I called my old high school youth pastor, Mark Teyler, and asked if he would meet with me. I remember vividly sitting in his office and sharing my story as he listened. He had been a pastor for over a decade, and after I was done, he looked me in the eye and said, "Brian, this is straight and simple an issue of your calling. You don't need the support of your senior pastor. You need the conviction of the Holy Spirit. You don't quit your calling when life gets tough. If you've been called to ministry, then it's time to search your soul, buck up, and deal with your discouragement. That's what Jeremiah had to do in chapter 20." My senior pastor was my comforter. My youth pastor was my confronter. The truth is, I desperately needed both.

As I huddled under my senior leader's wings and sought any kind of conviction from the Lord, I found solace and connection in Psalm 55. David cried out to God with these words: *If an enemy were insulting me, I could endure it; if a foe were rising against me, I could hide. But it is you, one like myself, my companion, my close friend, with whom I once enjoyed sweet fellowship at the house of God, as we walked about among the worshipers (Psalm 55:12-14 TNIV).* Perhaps harder than the criticism was the feeling of betrayal I felt in the midst of a group that I felt was so close. Trust was lost, and it was not due to a school district with a different ideology or a neighbor who didn't follow Jesus—I could understand those kinds of situations and even label them as from the enemy. But my spiritual dark hole was revolving around confusion in my calling and the death of a friendship in Christ. This seemed unbearable.

In the following six months, life only got worse. I did my first funeral when Scott, my father-in-law, died of a melanoma at 50 years old. Then my Grandpa Roger died and so did my wife's only living grandparent, "Gram." It was a deep season of soul searching and mourning that seemed to never end—both at home and at church. Through it, we didn't lose one other adult volunteer in our ministry, but our youth group lost about 50 percent of its students. Rumors were rampant, and students chose sides. I remember my wife looking at me one day and asking, "Are you ever going to be the same again?" I said to her, "I really don't know, and I'm not sure I want to."

It literally took a year before I got the confidence back to stand up again and consider taking another criticism bullet from anyone. John and I remained at the same church, but he no longer worked in the youth ministry. It took us several years and a lot of grace, but John and I eventually forgave one another and had our lives restored to a level of Christ-like brotherhood again. No, we would probably never be best friends, but we were again at a place of family in the kingdom of God.

With this shaping experience distantly in the rearview mirror, I can tell you that God was working in my life during those days. I would not wish them on anyone, but I'm not sure I would remove them from my story either. God clearly used those dark days of criticism to shape my life. I now understand what the author of Hebrews meant when he wrote this: *No discipline seems pleasant at the time, but painful. Later on, however, it produces a harvest of righteousness and peace for those who have been trained by it (Hebrews 12:11).* God truly used the men and women who loved God and loved me to shape me into who I am today. After almost 20 years as a youth pastor in just two churches, I've weathered many a storm that had the potential to knock out my passion for ministry, some storms more gracefully than others—but weathered nonetheless. I now confidently know this: In those days, God was refining my calling, sharpening my soul, and preparing me for the road ahead.

If you asked me to summarize that season of my life, I'd offer you the following conclusions.

- Remain broken so God doesn't have to break you. The fewer lessons you learn the hard way, the better off you'll be.

- The ability to deal with criticism is a mandatory life skill. We must learn to both ignore it from some and heed it from others.

- Without a clear calling from God, ministry longevity will never be a reality.

SOME QUESTIONS TO PONDER AS WE BEGIN THIS JOURNEY TOGETHER:

- What has been your most significant "criticism bites" moment to date? In other words, what life-shaping story would you tell if this were a chapter about a season of criticism in your life?

- What did you feel when that criticism came? If it's in your past, how did it shape you, and what lessons did you gain from it? If it's in your present, how are you responding, and how is it shaping you today?

- Who would you list as people who have cared enough to comfort and even confront you in seasons of discouragement in your own life?

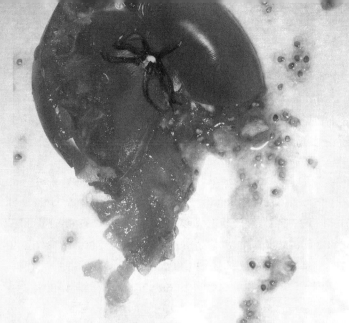

SECTION ONE

CRITICISM BITES— BUT WHY?

SEARCHING THE SOUL OF A LEADER

If you read about that season of my life and thought, "I love this stuff—criticism makes for such great stories," then put down this book and call your therapist. Something's wrong with you.

It is safe to assume that if we conducted a random research survey on criticism in street corners all over the country, everyone we interviewed would say they experience criticism, but no one would say they enjoy it or yearn for it. We'd find that even though conflict is normal, normal people don't enjoy conflict. However, just because you don't like it doesn't mean this can be passed off as an optional thing to master. Quite the opposite is true. If you're a leader of anything—a youth ministry, a school, a family, a church, a small group, a club, a team, a business, anything—then you will experience criticism. Your capacity to respond to criticism in ways that honor God is not an optional skill; it is a mandatory tool for all leaders. Ignoring it will set yourself up for failure and will cause the people and/or organization you lead to experience the negative effects of the funk you find yourself unable to navigate.

I also think that our survey would affirm one general observation about all people on the planet: Everyone is insecure. Yes, everyone. Maybe not about the same thing, but we're all insecure about something. Criticize them in that area and you'll find they immediately limp and hobble. It's like the Achilles' heel or the kryptonite of their soul. If you introduce criticism to this area of insecurity, it ruins them.

So to be a bit vulnerable with you, I'm insecure every time I speak in our main services. Perhaps it's because they're a lot bigger than youth group. Maybe it's because I know my boss is listening or, if he's out of town, eventually will listen to the podcast and will hear comments from those who heard it live—all of which are beyond my control. I even wonder if people will leave because the main speaker is not there. Maybe it's because I'm only on stage about three times a year and every time I feel like I have to hit a home run. But I also wonder if the offering will be big enough and if I'll be blamed for it if it's not. I wonder if my clothing is a distraction or if I'll look fat and balding on that big screen showing my image while I talk. I'm concerned about what impact this is having and if all three services will be equally done well. I'm my own walking insecurity blanket, and so is everyone else in the room—mine just happens to be held up in front of the world while I decide if it's safe or not for me to let you see it.

Think about it. You know the parents are wondering what people think of their kids' behavior. Women are comparing their bodies with others in the room. The men judged the experience and decided if they fit in or not within five minutes of stepping on the property. The single people are wondering if they're the only ones who are single, and if not, then what? A slew of habits and addictions came in the room with this crowd, and all are wondering if this is a safe place to drag out that baggage.

If into this sea of insecurity you begin to offer criticism, you will find that we all have things we care about and don't care about, and the degree to which we care is the degree to which your criticism will bite. So in order to respond wisely to our critics, we have to deal with our own issues. This is not just about your critics; it's about your own soul. Criticism is a two-way street, and we all must deal with our own insecurities in the process.

In addition, as I've talked with and watched people as they respond to criticism, I've discovered that it wrecks some more severely than others. We've all heard the cliché: "Sticks and stones can break my bones, but words can never hurt me." I could even name some people who seem to embody this bumper sticker and at least appear to be virtually immune to the critical words of others.

However, most people are not so immune. Within this group, we see two extremes and a thousand variations between them. On one end we find people who simply respond in anger, believing they are above anyone who might correct them. They are self-defensive, sarcastic, and quick to point out a critic's flaws before examining any error of their own ways. I have seen plenty of those responses and even have felt the temptation to be that kind of responder myself.

The other side of the pendulum is where you'll find people who are truly wounded by criticism but somehow respond with humility and health. They are honest, mature, self-controlled, teachable, and authentic in their emotions. They have discovered a much better way to deal with the criticism that sends many of us into action or into hiding to defend ourselves.

Regardless of our proximity to or distance from those responses, most people don't respond well, and there is no direct correlation between the ability to interact with one's critics and the volume of criticism one faces. In other words, receiving a boatload of criticism does not automatically create an ability to navigate it well any more than growing older means one is also growing up. Those who receive the most criticism—perhaps someone in the pop-culture limelight with the paparazzi following their every move—might also be the unhealthiest in how they respond to that barrage of criticism and personal invasion. The truth is, when anyone starts to accumulate a large amount of criticism, he or she quickly discovers that receiving it and being able to navigate it are not the same thing. This is a skill set we must intentionally grow, not an innate nature we can simply feed.

If you made a list of your least favorite things in the world to do, you'd find that everything you don't enjoy requires intentionality to tolerate doing—much less excel at doing. The lack of interest, almost by default, makes our investment in the betterment of the task at hand feel like a wasted investment. I mean, why bother getting better at what you hate to deal with? If criticism is on that list for you, then the ability to navigate it well is most likely motivated by desperation and intentionality, not joy.

For what it's worth, here's my quick list of stuff I hate to do:

1. Fire someone

2. Respond to a critical email from an irate parent

3. Spend all day in a meeting that has no real purpose, leaving me further behind than when I started

4. Listen to the sounds of people chewing to the beat of dub step

5. Go to the dentist

6. Itemize my credit card statement with all the right receipts and paperwork so I can turn it in for reimbursement at the church and pay my bill

7. Write a seminary research paper on Anselm's theory of atonement to sit in a file

8. Add more stuff to this depressing list

While your list will be different from mine, the universal question is not *what* is on the list, but *why* it is on the list. To this end, we all must wrestle with this question: "Why do I dislike criticism so much?" If we each knew why it hurts and why we personally don't enjoy it, we could see the root cause more clearly and then know how to rightly address it.

For example, take an item on my "stuff I hate" list: the dentist. I hate going to the dentist because they always criticize something I'm doing or not doing and charge me ridiculous amounts of money to deliver this criticism. I'm not a fan. However, without fail, every time I go into the dentist, they also want to take an X-ray of my teeth to see what the problems are from a photographic vantage point. Even though I don't look forward to what I'll likely hear, I still understand the need for an X-ray before they start drilling on my face. In a similar way, we can wisely take a cue from the dentists of the world, and before we start digging for solutions to dealing with and responding to our critics, we must correctly identify the real reasons criticism bites so much.

So to this end, I encourage you to wrestle with me in this question: **"Why is criticism so painful?"** Please read that question again. I'm not asking you to give it the head nod and mental agreement you might have given to the "criticism is not fun" concept. So if you read it fast and thought, "Yeah, why *is* criticism so painful?", please read it again and ask, **"Oh God, please show me why criticism is so painful."** With this in mind, I ask you to read these next five chapters inviting the Holy Spirit to show you specifically which root issues make criticism unbearable for you at times. We don't want to know why it is so for all police officers or teachers or even Christ-followers in general. This is not about why it's so tough for your senior pastor or for me as an author or for the most annoying person in your ministry who won't listen to you. The question is "What makes it hard for YOU?"

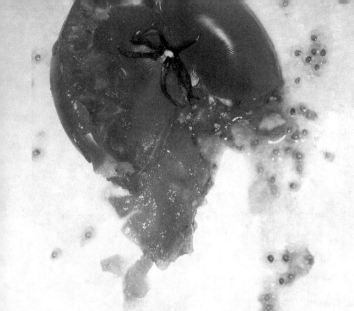

CHAPTER 2
AN IDENTITY
CRISIS

WHEN OUR IDENTITY AND OUR WORK ARE INSEPARABLY WOVEN TOGETHER

How does it feel as a leader when someone tells you, "I'm not being fed in small groups," or when your senior pastor says, "I'm concerned that the youth group is not doing enough events during the summer"? How does it feel as a parent when someone criticizes your kid on a sports field? How does it feel as a business owner when someone gives your business a critical review online? I mean beyond the point where your blood pressure rose, you gritted your teeth, and you choked down the 40 things you wanted to say or write to them in defense and response. I mean, "What did it feel like on a soul level?" For me, the answer is: It feels like that person criticized me and that I am the problem.

But in all those cases, the criticism isn't even specifically about me (or you). It was your kid who kicked the ball in a way that the other person criticized. It was the business that got the review. It was about a small group and event structure that someone was unhappy with, not a talk you gave or even a flier you personally designed. But in my life, the things I do and associate with are never distantly related to me. It's never *just* my kid. It's never *just* my work. It's never *just* an event we planned. My life and the things I lead are *deeply* rooted and tied to who I am. When my family bleeds, I bleed. When my ministry fails, I fail. When it wins, I win. As a Christ-follower, the things I do are a calling, and regardless of whether I'm paid or not, criticism bites, in part, because I can't separate my life work from my soul. They are seemingly inseparable.

On the one side, this seems right and noble. You should have a high level of ownership with the things you do—especially if it's your ministry's reputation or the character of your family. But this is not about ownership, it's about identity—and while the difference may seem subtle, it's massively significant. The question is this: "Is our identity supposed to be intimately tied with our achievement?" I think the answer to this holds a truth many of us need to hear so we can listen to our critics without being knocked out by them.

Here's the brutal truth in answer to that question: NO. As Christ-followers, our identity is in Jesus. Period. This is why the Apostle Paul wrote these words: *I have been crucified with Christ and I no longer live, but Christ lives in me. The life I now live in the body, I live by faith in the Son of God, who loved me and gave himself for me (Galatians 2:20).* In other words, at the center of the gospel is an identity change. You and I were called to be children of God. *Then* we were called to embrace the calling of a parent or profession. God has not called you to BE the ministry at your church. He has not called you to BE the business you own or the profession you chose. He's called each of us to BE a follower of Jesus and to DO life in the world. When we accepted that call, we agreed to ditch the former identity of our achievements for the real identity of Christ. That's how Paul could dismiss his achievement pile as mere rubbish or garbage (Philippians 3:8). If my work is rubbish compared with my identity in Christ, then when someone criticizes my achievements or work, it's like complaining about my garbage pile. How ridiculous is that? My achievements really don't amount to much, yet I feel so much ownership of them that I get deeply wounded when others don't like them.

There's no way around it: My *being* and my *doing* are both radically different and intimately connected. But order matters. My being must lead to my doing. First being. Then doing. When we get the order reversed, the pain of criticism increases exponentially. So when I exchange my primary identity as a child of God for a primary identity of pastor, it affects my doing in some profound ways—not the least of which is when I take criticism of my ministry as a personal attack on my soul. This, however, is less a sign that I own my ministry and more a sign of a lack of health. When we do this with our life work, we have an identity confusion issue we must address.

Jesus himself cautioned that doing stuff in life without first being in God is lifeless and pointless. In the Sermon on the Mount, he warns that it is possible to do some amazing things, but to have them ultimately be declared unauthorized and empty of the Spirit (Matthew 7:21-23). The story of the prodigal son in Luke 15, while often highlighted as an illustration of God's heart for people who are spiritually lost, is also about identity confusion for the older brother, who thought his doing earned him more credit with the father. When the older brother finds out that this isn't how it works and that the father misses his faithless son as much as he enjoys the presence of his faithful son, the older brother leaves in a huff and refuses to celebrate his lost brother's repentance or his father's joy. He thinks his achievement pile deserves a larger reward. It has become his identity. So while the older brother was physically *living* much closer to his father, he was not actually *with his father* any more than his distant and rebellious brother was. Despite all the older brother had done for the father, in the end he was just as far—if not farther—from his dad as his brother who left for another land. This is both a tragedy and a warning to those of us who have become so consumed in our doing that it has begun to shape our soul.

Recently I was reminded that the baptism of Jesus has some profound implications for us in this, too. Before Jesus had done one miracle, before he had gone anywhere or invited anyone to follow him or been called "Rabbi" or "Messiah" by anyone, this happened: *And a voice came from heaven: "You are my Son, whom I love; with you I am well pleased" (Mark 1:11).* At this point in the biblical record, the brutal truth is that Jesus had done zippola publically in the way of ministry. He was scandalously born to a virgin, had a moment when he was 12 that made the record when he amazed some people with wisdom beyond his years, and then evidently lived in relative obscurity until the day he was baptized in his early 30s. But in spite of this little-to-no track record for building a worthy résumé, in that moment the Father reminds the Son that his identity is "one with whom I am well pleased." Notice that the voice didn't say, "I love you because you're an awesome and awe-inspiring teacher." It wasn't because Jesus had picked the best small group of 12 the Father had ever seen. It wasn't because of anything Jesus did or would do, but because of who he was (and is). In some crazy, complicated, Trinitarian way, the communal oneness of God is at peace, and Jesus—in his humanity and on the brink of his public ministry—is reminded by the Father that this is not an achievement game. "You don't have to turn every rock into bread or cure every disease. Just be who you are and do what I've called you to do. That's enough. No more, no less."

Similarly, the Apostle Paul offered this reminder to the church in Ephesus: *For it is by grace you have been saved, through faith—and this is not from yourselves, it is the gift of God—not by works, so that no one can boast. For we are God's handiwork, created in Christ Jesus to do good works, which God prepared in advance for us to do (Ephesians 2:8-10).* You might even have those verses memorized, but have you absorbed the truth of that Scripture? Knowing that I'm saved by grace and that God is pleased with me simply because of Christ in me ought to give me some latitude when someone criticizes my ministry. It should remind me that I don't have to get my ego all in the way as if my work, my family, my athletic ability, or anything else is the epicenter of my life. They are not the epicenter. God is.

Yes, Jesus called you and me, like Peter, to be a crucial member of the body of Christ. But let's not forget who is in charge—especially if you're a pastor at a church. We must remember that it is God who is building HIS church—not you or me building OUR little kingdoms. He's been doing this since LONG before we were born and will be doing it LONG after we're done. Notice carefully what Jesus said to Peter: *"And I tell you that you are Peter, and on this rock I will build my church, and the gates of Hades will not overcome it" (Matthew 16:18).* Jesus is the one building the church. He's the one building the body of Christ into his people, regardless of your profession or the status of your family. To endure criticism, you and I have to let Jesus lead. When I insist that someone's criticism of my achievement or something I have a deep ownership of directly reflects me, I've got some work to do.

By way of confession, I recently felt like God reminded me that this is still an issue that I have not yet mastered. It happened on a full-day spiritual retreat for our pastoral team. It really was a great day, facilitated by a spiritual director named Larry Warner,[3] who our church had hired to work with us to "keep the main thing the main thing." The premise is basically that the healthier the spiritual life of our pastoral team, the healthier our leadership, teaching, and influence will therefore be. To this end, one of the things we were supposed to do was spend several hours in the afternoon processing a packet that Larry had put together. However, I never really got into the packet because I got stuck on this sentence I found in the introduction. He wrote that in our culture, "Our value flows from what we own, what we do, and what significant others think of us. Today we seek to begin to embrace our God-given identity."

As I read it, it sounded like it was in bold print from God to me. I asked myself this: "If someone stripped away everything I owned, everything I've done, and the value I feel because certain influential people happen to like something I've done—how big of a pile would I have left?" I didn't really like the answer. For me, this realization again reminded me how far I still have to go in this. As long as I continue to find my worth in what I own, what I do, and what others think of me, I will maintain an unhealthy level of ownership and funk attached to the critical comments of others.

If this is your situation, too, let me invite you to wrestle this one to the ground. The roles you embrace and profession you choose are part of your calling from God. Don't let them subtly become your God.

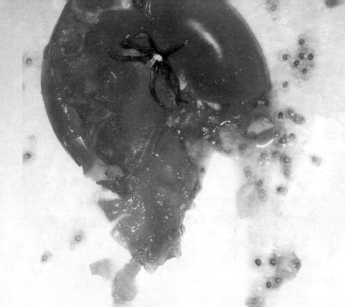

CHAPTER 3
THERE'S A PRICE TAG ATTACHED

THE UNSPOKEN BAGGAGE OF A PAYCHECK

If you're not paid to do a job that generates some of your criticism, then you can skip this chapter. But if you are, regardless of the size of your paycheck, this factor adds weight to and taints your perspective on criticism. If a neighbor criticizes you because your yard looks like a scene from an apocalypse movie, perhaps you can laugh it off because you're horrible at yard work. I have some friends with the last name of Taylor, and when their yard's weed height and the pile of broken misfit cars begin to reflect how full their lives are, they just laugh it off and call themselves "Taylor Trash." They find the room to not care, in part because it's not their "job."

You might be a horrible landscaper yet still be amazing at tons of other things. If you're a great teacher but you're inept at lawn care, it really doesn't matter. You can simply hire someone who is amazing at landscaping—or call yourself the slacker of your neighborhood and ignore it. It's not your job, and both you and the public in general can give yourself permission to be mediocre or even terrible at it.

If someone criticizes my ability to do something that is not tied to a paycheck, it often holds very little weight in my world. In the "sticks and stones" cliché, these words are like "twigs and pebbles." They simply don't hurt that bad because I don't need to be awesome at them to rest peacefully at night. However, if someone is not connecting with my ministry or doesn't like the events we've planned, then there's more weight to it because it's part of my job. And regardless of your profession, when a critical comment is tied to what funds the house payment, your family's needs, groceries, a spouse, the electrical bill, and the like, don't underestimate the weight added by that connection.

As someone who works in the church, which by definition is a largely volunteer-run organization, I find that this one really bugs me—especially if someone who decided to serve in our church or a student who comes to my ministry criticizes something and eventually ends up leaving altogether. I feel like they just trashed my office and then left me to clean up the mess. But I don't have this same luxury to leave. I don't get to decide that the mess is too big and just walk away in search of some new church. I don't have the option of making a stink and then just up and leaving. Yes, I know this is about my calling. But it's also more complicated than that when a paycheck is involved.

For example, I feel a calling from God to be involved in coaching my kids' soccer teams right now. But if I don't like the way the soccer club is run, I can still coach by finding another organization to work with—and taking my kids with me if I want to. Yes, I also could stay and try to help solve the problem, but as a volunteer, I have the freedom to leave and not help solve the real problem if I don't want to. This is why customer service matters to employers so much. People have choices for where they buy their goods and services, and if they don't like your store, they can just go elsewhere. To you as a consumer, it's your right. To the business owner, it's not that simple. If enough people negatively review their business product, they go out of business. This is how some people treat volunteering at church. If something isn't being done right, they just up and quit—and like a good consumer, go church shopping. Though I think this come-and-go-when-you-want-to mindset is a grave error in what it means for us to be a community of Christ-followers, the point I'm making remains true: A paycheck complicates things.

Let's be honest enough to admit that jobs are not that easy to replace and therefore criticism tied to them becomes loaded, regardless of the industry. In youth ministry, if a critical comment goes viral or an opinion holds enough weight, I might lose my job and have to move my family. Maybe it's a long shot, but I've seen it happen, and the same might be true for you, too.

Perhaps this sounds cheap or worldly to you, like no good pastor would ever let a paycheck get in the way of a criticism. Perhaps you're right. Maybe it is worldly. But so are divorce, adultery, and greed—and all of those, if left unchecked, can knock and have knocked many people out of ministry and destroyed many marriages. Sadly, just because something is worldly does not mean it is powerless.

Speaking of marriage, while there is no "paycheck" per se in that relationship, there is something significant that makes criticism tough in similar ways. Because there is a contract you've both signed with social, moral, and financial implications for leaving it, this also adds weight to criticism. When two become one flesh, it heightens the implications when someone criticizes one's marriage or spouse. Because you're "stuck" with the one you married, criticism of them or the two of you bites harder.

There are no two ways around it: External factors affect the ownership and depth of which I let criticism bite me. Both my marriage and my work have other factors that change my perspective, and if I'm going to deal with criticism wisely, I have to have enough self-awareness to turn and face the hidden implications that come with it.

In terms of a paycheck, this is not a chapter in defense of your contract or what you should get paid for the amount of junk you take along the way. This is simply the theological equivalent of a "Caution: Slippery When Wet" floor sign. If you've been working for any length of time, then you know plenty of people who have lost their jobs due to the remarks of a powerful and critical boss or leader. If you've been *in ministry* for any length of time, then you know of people who have left due to the stink caused by an elder, volunteer, or key family. I'm not trying to offer credibility to their remarks; I'm simply saying that if you're taking a paycheck, when criticism comes, by default it is loaded and must be handled with caution. It must be carefully sorted through, and you must call out the elephant in the room. Failure is not an option, and if the criticism is significant enough and supported by enough others with influence, it could spell trouble.

This came up once in my life when a pair of Mormon missionaries came into my neighborhood. I was out front working on my truck when they asked me if I needed any help. I said, "No thanks," and they went along their way to knock on another door. But due to the layout of our streets, after doing their route, they had to pass my house a second time, and when they did, they found me still working—and again asked if I needed any help. Even though I denied them a second time, they continued to persist until finally, hoping to get them to leave, I said, "I really don't need your help today. But in two days I'm starting a massive remodel project at my house, and if you want to lose the ties and come back then, I could use your help." It worked. They said, "OK" and left.

I didn't think much of the exchange at the time. But much to my surprise, two days later, while I was ripping out a bathroom, I heard the doorbell ring. When I opened it, these same two guys were standing on my porch in T-shirts with badges. "We lost the ties, and we're here to help," they said. I just laughed and said, "Yes, you did; come on in." They worked hard for hours without complaining, and then they told me they had to get going.

I thanked them for their help and in exchange, knowing they wanted to talk, offered to sit with them for a half-hour and drink some lemonade. But as we sat down and before they started with questions, I told them that I needed to be straight with them. "I'm thankful for your help today and you've surely earned the opportunity to explore my beliefs," I said. "But you need to know that I'm a high school youth pastor at a church across town, and if in the next 30 minutes one of us convinces the other that we've bought a lie, we're in a lot of trouble. If I'm wrong, and I decide to convert to Mormonism, then I'm gonna lose my job and this remodel project is not getting finished and my family and I are going to have to move into my parents' garage. If you're wrong, and I convince you that something you believe is not true, then you will have to go home and explain a lot of stuff to your parents and the bishop who sent you on this mission in the first place. So there's a lot on the line in this conversation." Needless to say, our conversation didn't last too long or go very far—there simply was too much on the line.

The same is true when someone criticizes something that you depend on for financial security. Unlike the issues of identity in Christ where something needs to be fixed in us, this is more of the "tension to manage" variety. As long as you receive a paycheck, this will be true. But when we call it out, we can at least sort through some of the other factors that play into this. Especially if you are financially stretched and the economy has you living paycheck to paycheck, don't underestimate the influence that can have on your ability to navigate criticism in healthy ways. Don't let the fact that you're a paid employee or the primary bread winner of your home give someone's comments an exorbitant amount of energy or turn the criticism back into an identity issue. Your role as employee is not your primary identity any more than the place you get your paycheck should be.

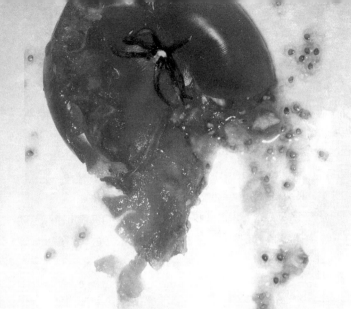

CHAPTER 4
COMPAREANOIA

THE OLDEST GAME IN THE WORLD

From time to time I have students in my ministry that are involved in other churches. Sometimes it's because they have divorced parents who attend different places and we get them based on whose weekend it is. Other times it's because the other church has no youth group. Still other times, it's because of where their friends go, the event they're putting on, and more fickle teenage reasons. Regardless of the motive, as a leader of our local network of youth ministries, I know most of their youth pastors, and we are essentially friends who can even pastor them together to some degree.

So most of the time I'm able to ignore it, but occasionally, this multi-church thing produces conflicts. The latest one for me was a student whose dad doesn't go to church at all but whose mom attends our church. She has two teenage sons, both of whom are involved in our ministry to some degree, though the older of the two usually goes to midweek small groups at another church. He also goes to their summer camp instead of ours, and he just kind of drops in from time to time when it feels good for him.

This past fall, I saw him for the first time in a long time because he'd been gone all summer. So that weekend, I told him he was missed, went out of my way to make sure he knew he was welcome, and teased him a little that I hoped it wouldn't be Christmas when I saw him again. (Ha ha, smiles, and laughter.) Later that day, after I got home from church, I got this email from his mom:

I was saddened today to hear from [my older son] that he will probably not be returning to your small groups or Sunday services. He is feeling like he is teased when he does come or if he misses a function. He told me in confidence that when he goes to [insert the name of the bigger church down the road here, where he attends most midweek events], they always make him feel wanted and glad that he is there, without teasing or making him feel guilty that he missed something.

I'll spare you my reaction and just say: I hate emails like this. I don't like responding to criticism via email, so I usually try to set up a face-to-face meeting or at least a phone call instead. But whether I attempt an email or arrange an appointment, before I respond, I have to call out some stuff inside me. Yes, there is always a desire to defend myself and share my side of the story, which usually comes off as defensive. There's the part of me that wants to go on the offensive and return criticism with criticism. But in cases like this one, there's the comparison factor, too.

If we can admit that something in this email unleashes a jealous thread about the perceived better youth group down the street, then we also have to admit that we have a spiritually diagnosable disease I call "compareanoia," and it complicates everything—especially the words of your critics. Somewhere inside, we wish we had the natural ability, the skill set, the creativity, the likeability, the resources—pretty much anything we feel that we lack but that we see in our friends, our co-workers, another family, another team, another church, or another business. When we don't have what we think they have, we make excuses for why we didn't see the results they did, blame some kind of favoritism they got from God, and say that if we had such and such, we could do that, too. In the end, it's just a big comparison game that leaves us feeling like we are on top of the world if we compare ourselves to "someone we are better than"—or like a total loser if we compare ourselves to someone with "the success we want." Now into that sea of ridiculousness enters criticism. Is it any wonder that it would contribute to not navigating it well?

We might find some solace in knowing we're not the first ones with this problem, even though we clearly should not rest here. The Scriptures give us evidence that this comparison game is not a new thing on the landscape of the world and neither are the grave consequences of not managing this tension well. In fact, it's a mere four chapters into Genesis when Cain kills his brother Abel because of the criticism of his offering and not his brother's. As the comparison game enters the story and begins to rear its ugly head, Cain feels rejected by God, inferior to his brother, and irreconcilably angry, so he solves the comparison problem with the first murder in human history. This extreme evidence of evil is directly tied to Cain's inability to navigate any correction—even from God himself—due to the foundational problem of comparison gone bad. Even when God tells Cain that all he has to be is faithful with what he has, it's not enough for Cain. The criticism of his offering is more than he can bear because he has a comparison complex.

Perhaps this is why coveting made God's top 10 list when he chiseled it on stone tablets and gave it to Moses. *"You shall not covet your neighbor's house. You shall not covet your neighbor's wife, or his male or female servant, his ox or donkey, or anything that belongs to your neighbor" (Exodus 20:17).* In other words, stop comparing yourself with everyone around you. It made the same list as "don't murder" and "don't commit adultery"—neither of which is permitted as "normal" behavior by Christ-followers today. However, we've made allowances for coveting, and it impacts how we respond to our critics. If you're constantly comparing yourself with the married couple and thinking your problem is that you're single, then you're going to slash back when someone rips into your dating life. If you're comparing your paycheck with the paycheck of others on your staff or the employer next door, don't be surprised if you lose it when someone offers a criticism on how your last budget went. When the comparison game is alive and well, it wrecks havoc on our ability to respond to our critics.

Fast-forward in the Bible to the life of King Saul, and we see something similar. After God told Samuel that Saul had been rejected as Israel's king, Samuel went to the house of Jesse in search of his successor. When he arrived, he thought the first son he saw must surely be God's chosen. However, God reminded Samuel that unlike most people, God does not look at the world through the comparison lens. God peers past our external comparison games and into the real issues of our heart. This is why the Lord told Samuel, *"Do not consider his appearance or his height, for I have rejected him. The Lord does not look at the things people look at. People look at the outward appearance, but the Lord looks at the heart"* (1 Samuel 16:7).

We would do well to remind ourselves of this. God is not into the comparison of people. We are not graded on a scale or in some sort of cosmic game in which we try to outdo the others on the planet. Each of us will be judged for how we handled what God has given us, not how we handled it compared with another pastor, church, small group leader, Christ-follower, parent, volunteer, or business owner.

Plain and simple, it would appear that the comparison game is rooted in evil. Not a great place to dwell.

Once Saul discovers that God has left him and sees God's favor on David, his first instinct echoes Cain's decision: try to kill David. He makes several attempts, all directly tied to his own compareanoia. Saul becomes angry when the women of the towns compare how many men Saul has killed with how many David has killed and put it to song—singing, *"Saul has slain his thousands, and David his tens of thousands." Saul was very angry; this refrain displeased him greatly.* Then verse 9 reveals a bone-chilling truth: *And from that time on Saul kept a close eye on David (1 Samuel 18:7-9).* Saul didn't have his eyes on God; he had his eyes on a comparison game he thought he was losing to David, and in the end it drove him literally insane—so much so that the Scriptures tell us that Saul's jealousy made him David's *enemy the rest of his days (1 Samuel 18:29).* Saul went from king to enemy of the future king, all because of comparison.

This could be our story, too, if we don't say no to the two-column comparison model of life—the way we tend to pit ourselves against others by deciding how well we're doing based on some crazy scale that evaluates our abilities versus theirs. It might look like this:

	ME	THEM
AGE and GENDER	40, male	28, male
PAY and EXPERIENCE	$$, 20 years	$$$, 5 years
ACHIEVEMENT and SUCCESS	Wrote a book	Wrote a book that actually sold a bunch of copies
REPUTATION and INFLUENCE	Husband, dad, pastor	Husband, church planter, speaker
POSSESSIONS and STUFF	House in San Diego and a dog	Personal jet and a race horse

If you're doing this in your head with someone else or some group of other people, then let me encourage you to go back to the drawing board and erase it. When we hold on to it, and someone criticizes our column, we get ruined because we were already losing this made-up and evil comparison game.

Maybe your critics are right. Maybe you don't do something as well as the next guy or gal down the street. Maybe you're a great shepherd but a lousy administrator. Or maybe you're an awesome communicator and a horrible grief counselor. So what? Seriously, maybe somebody needs to give you permission to just get over it. You're not them. It is time that we call out this stuff as a lie. We need to stop comparing our weaknesses with others' strengths and our strengths with their weaknesses.

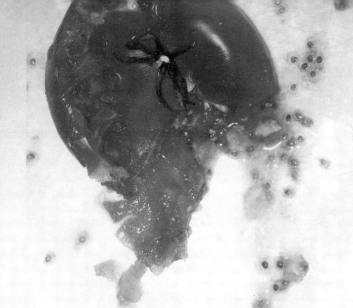

CHAPTER 5
THE MYTH
OF SUCCESS

WHEN WE ONLY CELEBRATE A "WIN"

The outreach didn't work. You're a failure.

The meeting bombed. You're a loser.

That talk you gave was flat. You should quit teaching.

Your team lost because you called the wrong play. It's all your fault.

For a second, let's assume that all the first statements of those sentence pairs are absolutely true. Your outreach didn't reach anyone. Your volunteer meeting was not good. Your talk left plenty of room for improvement in your teaching technique. You did call the wrong play, and it did cost your team the game. Even if that's all true, one reason we can't stand to hear any of that is because there's a period after the sentence. We said it. The result was not good. Period. This kind of thinking naturally results in the second set of statements. We feel demoralized, we label ourselves failures, and we ponder quitting. This is because in our culture we celebrate success as a win, but the process gets no glory, and setbacks are deemed failures.

I once dropped a $5,000 projector from a ceiling onto a concrete floor when getting it down to take to summer camp. Let's just say that projector had a lot in common with Humpty Dumpty.

Speaking of summer camp, I left a teenager there once. Oh, he got on the bus. But then he got *off* the bus to go to the bathroom. We left him three hours from home. It was long before the days of cell phones where he would have called a friend to alert us. So I just drove the bus home. Never knew he wasn't on it until we got back and then had to send his parents 30 minutes away to get him from the people at the other church from our camp who had found him and brought him home for us. Awesome.

I also made up a game for camp. We were gonna wrestle pigs. Just like in the movies, but for city kids who never do this stuff. So I got a pig from a farm. Built a fence enclosure. Covered the pig in Crisco®. Told it to run. It just stood there as four kids ran to it. When they got there, it squealed loud like a little girl being tortured. The girls cried. The pig peed. It was supposed to take an hour. It lasted five minutes and got me labeled as an animal hater. It took me weeks and weeks to prepare and plan for what was a total failure.

So I learned from my mistake and made up a different game another year: human bowling. It had real bowling pins set up on the gym floor, a kid with a helmet on a furniture cart being propelled by friends holding giant bungee cords, and "epicness" written all over it. It evidently also had "concussion" written on it because a 90-pound freshman girl FLEW on the thing—and instead of falling off the cart or putting up her hands, she just put her head down and like an angry bull straight plowed right through the pins and went headfirst into a wall.

She survived. I didn't get sued. God is good. My game-planning skills evidently are not.

When I moved to San Diego we had two services for students on Sunday mornings: one at 8:30 a.m. and one at 10 a.m. The 8:30 a.m. service was three times larger than the 10 a.m. one. Go figure. The handful that came to the 10 a.m. seemed to hate church, Jesus, me, my dog, and doing anything except staring blankly at me. I really wanted them to just cuss me out so we could have a real conversation about something they did care about, but they didn't. Every week I would walk into the utility closet in the back of our room between services and stare at myself in the mirror over the sink. At 35 years old, I'd give myself a pep talk and say, "You can do it. You can do it. You can do it." And then I would walk out and smile and give 110 percent to what I affectionately called "preaching to the detention center."

After doing this for over a year and quitting every Sunday as I walked back to my office (before I re-hired myself on Tuesday morning), I finally pitched to my senior pastor that we should ditch the 8:30 a.m. service and move all of the students to 10:30—a much more realistic, normalish hour for teenagers to be awake on a Sunday. I thought this would help me outnumber the haters at 10:30, and since I had to have two service options, we could then start a 6 p.m. service on Sunday that I hoped to grow (and I secretly prayed it would get so large we could do nothing but the 6 p.m. service). Well, the 6 p.m. service started with a bang but then proceeded to slowly die until I had to call it a failure and cancel it a year later.

Do I need to keep going? This is getting painful.

Through all of that, over the course of 19 years, I've served in two ministries as a youth pastor. I served for 11 years in one in Northern California and have been in my current ministry context for eight years. Along the way, I've clearly amassed plenty of failure stories. But if we want to have any kind of longevity in leadership, we can't limit the word success to only those things we think went well. Success is not about an event that goes right. Sure, that's a form of success—but not if that means you're done or that if it didn't go well, you're a failure. It's about a much bigger and much larger goal. For me, I need to remind myself that I'm trying to "invite a generation to understand, own, and live out a life-changing faith in Jesus." My ultimate goal is not to plan great talks and perfect retreats, even though they're helpful. I want success, but if the ultimate goal I have is a God-sized goal, then it's not going to happen in one event or meeting, and I should expect some failures, setbacks, and even legitimate criticism along the way. If you put a "period" after every experience, this will kill you. We need to accept the fact that a failed talk, a bad decision, or an event we deem a flop does not mean we're a failure. It means we have some things to learn and now we can be wiser for it.

Consider this advice from the University of Oregon on its Holden Leadership Center website:

> Admit your mistakes and examine them carefully. Take responsibility for them, and learn from them. Mistakes are superb teachers. Knowing what doesn't work, can be a tremendous help in determining what will work.
>
> Tom Watson, the founder of IBM, well understood the value of mistakes. Once, one of his employees made a huge mistake that cost the company millions of dollars. The employee, upon being called into Watson's office, said "I suppose you want my resignation." "Are you kidding," replied Watson. "I just spent ten million dollars educating you."
>
> Successful, effective people learn from everything that happens, including mistakes. When you make a mistake, the best policy is to pick up the pieces and look carefully at what happened. Don't tear yourself up over it. Just examine it and learn from it. Then apply your new knowledge and try again.[4]

That's great advice. But it's only advice we can hear if we're willing to step away from the idea of "success" as an end product that our culture loves to worship. As one of my friends says, "Anything worth doing is worth doing poorly." He's simply saying that if we're called to do it, then we can take some criticism and do it badly—because the point is not how well we did that thing, but that we kept the main thing the main thing and we're in process on it. That's better than being people who quit because we couldn't do it well enough to get the loudest applause. If we take criticism as the final word on us, we won't be able to deflect, accept, or hear any critical commentary without it crushing us.

If this is you, find some encouragement in the life of Peter. He's your best friend in Scripture for giving you some hope. Stew on this: The dude was once called "Satan" by Jesus, then he moved up on the "good disciple list," only to cut off a soldier's ear and get rebuked by Jesus for his reckless zeal. He then denied Jesus multiple times, chucked it all and went back to fishing, and was confronted for legalism by Paul in a letter and by God in a dream. Yet he still walked on water with Jesus while his buddies watched in fear, preached a sermon on Pentecost that resulted in thousands becoming followers of Jesus, wrote two letters enclosed in the New Testament, and became a founder of the church of which both you and I are now a downstream beneficiary. Yes, you might have messed up along the way. But relax; you're not a failure. That criticism is not the last word. Don't let it define you. Let it shape you.

I remember a day early on in youth ministry when I came home late from youth group and plopped down in front of the TV around 11 p.m. I turned it on, trying to drown out the feelings of being a failure because the night had not gone well at all. I began to wonder if this roller coaster I called youth ministry had so many ups and downs in it—maybe I was in the wrong job.

While all that is rolling through my head and the song of failure was on repeat, David Letterman begins his monologue. And it's bombing. So he tries to revive it—and it's still bombing. No one is laughing. Lines are falling flat. The "LAUGH" cue cards aren't even causing the audience to giggle. Finally he pauses to ask his sidekick, Paul Shaffer, "How many shows do you think we do in a year?" Shaffer says something like, "I don't know, 200 or so." To which Letterman asks, "That's a lot, right?" Shaffer says, "Yep, that's a lot," and then Letterman does the math and says, "Wow, I've been on this show telling jokes for 20 years, so that makes for thousands of times." Then he walks up to the camera, sticks his face in the screen, stares straight into my eyes, and says, "Hey, kids. You can't be good all the time"—and walks away laughing.

I just sat there dumbfounded. I couldn't believe it. God just spoke to me through David Letterman. I began to understand that Letterman's ability to call out a failure for what it is and move on was a God thing. It allows people to find true success and peace in the midst of criticism. If you can't label something broken, then there's a good chance you have a end-product-only view of success, and you'll likely try to hide from view anything that doesn't go right. If you start literally shoving things under the carpet and getting tattoos to cover up scars, you're in this deep.

Success is not a goal we worship; it is a process we embrace. As we look to that process to bring us to our goal, our critics will come and go—and because it's not all on the line all the time, it won't be the end of us.

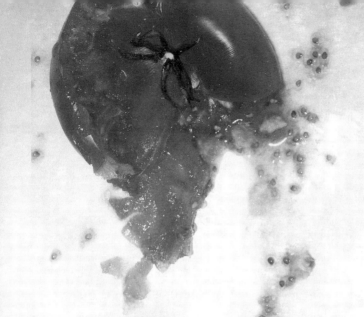

CHAPTER 6
I CAN DO IT...
NO I CAN'T

WHEN INDIVIDUALISM AND BUSYNESS BECOME OUR GOD, CRITICISM IS OUR ENEMY

"I can do it."

"I got this thing."

"You can count on me."

"Just give me the chance; I'll prove it to you."

All of these statements are prevalent in our culture and reflect a basic American idea that you should be able to do stuff yourself. We are a do-it-yourself society, and perhaps more than any other chapter in this book, this one is directed at me. Being brutally honest with you, I find myself here a lot.

With the addition of YouTube® to the cultural mix, you can learn pretty much anything you want via a tutorial, if you have the desire and enough time. My kids have learned how to make duct tape wallets, play instruments, and build paracord bracelets. Thanks to a YouTube video, I figured out that you have to remove the wheel to change the headlight on my PT Cruiser™. (Yup, remove the stupid wheel. Go figure. The engineer was clearly not planning on owning the car. No wonder I couldn't figure it out.)

I once repaired a battery-operated Nerf® gun by watching a YouTube video of a guy who had fixed the same problem. I found a website (ifixit. com) that has free step-by-step instructions (with pictures) on how to repair both my iPhone® screen and my wife's MacBook® track pad. It's like having a computer tech over your shoulder telling you what to do at every turn. Why would I hire someone or search for someone to do it, when I can do it myself?

This is both good and bad.

If you're not careful, you'll start to accept this cultural assumption in every area of your life and believe that you should be able to singlehandedly do it all. In youth ministry, it goes something like this: A good youth worker can play a guitar, preach a sermon, build a website, prepare a meal for 50, lead a small group, write curriculum, drive a bus, shoot and edit videos, plan retreats, be the janitor, run a campus club, be a surrogate parent to every student with a single-parent home, and accomplish about 5,000 other things all at the same time. But if you put that crazy list of me-centered ministry expectations in your coffee and drink it, don't be surprised when criticism rocks your world. When someone criticizes something on that ludicrous list of spinning plates, it will crash to the ground and you'll be picking up the pieces while feeling like a failure again. It's the default consequence of an "it's all about me" world where every flaw in the system is mine alone to own.

This ridiculous idea finally clicked for me one morning at 4 a.m. Yup, 4 a.m. No, I wasn't in bed. I was at church. No, it wasn't a youth group all-nighter. I gave those up long ago for my sanity's sake. No one should be allowed to do those things. Instead, I was at church setting up for youth group in honor of a different kind of insanity: the "I can do it all" insanity.

We had a new series and a new set design planned where the room would reflect the new teaching theme. We've done tons of these, but this time it wasn't done. The room was a mess from our half-done set design and a homeless ministry prep thing that happened on Friday night. Honestly, it looked like someone had ransacked the place; some chairs were even broken. I knew it was like this because I had come in the room after the Friday service at church and saw that the room was completely undone. But I was wiped and I decided I'd just come in at 4 a.m. on Sunday to finish it.

So I was walking around the room with a cordless drill, fixing stuff alone when I heard this voice ask me, "What are you doing?" Maybe it was only in my head, but it sounded like it was from the heavens. I turned around but no one was there. Just God and me, and evidently he had only one question: "What are you doing?" My answer? "Everything!" I said.

I *was* doing everything: making projector slides, cleaning up the room, painting signs, fixing chairs, writing messages, preparing the outline, making copies, sweeping the floor, and setting up the computer. In angst, I said to God, "What am I supposed to do? I mean, I'm not the senior pastor and I don't have a team of 10 paid people to do everything I don't have time to do. When was the last time my boss was in the building at 4 a.m. fixing anything?" God's answer to my rant? Just silence. It was like God left me in my own rambling complaint to ponder the neck-deep mess I was in.

As I explained this scenario later to a few trusted friends and confessed that I was at the end of my sanity rope, they asked me just one question: "Why didn't you call us and ask for help?" I looked at them and said, "Because it was 4 a.m." They said, "Oh, we see; friends only help friends in a bind in convenient times." Ouch. I had been at church at 4 a.m. working hard and ranting about it to God—and the truth is, I was alone because I chose to be, not because God designed me to be.

In one of his letters to the Corinthian church, Paul reminded this ragtag group of believers from all different walks of life that they were not called to be it all or do it all. They were called to be a part of the body of Christ. Read the word *part* as very important—not just any part either, but a specific part assigned to them by one God for one purpose: the common good. *Now to each one the manifestation of the Spirit is given for the common good....Now you are the body of Christ, and each one of you is a part of it (1 Corinthians 12:7, 27).* I think that for some of us, this is one of the bedrock reasons criticism stings so deeply. If we walk around feeling like we should be able to do it all for everyone, we'll begin trying to be the prosthetic limb for all the parts of the body that are not working right. Plain and simple, we'll think this is our job because we have given ourselves no permission to write anything off as "not my job" or "not my calling."

Here's what I've heard some people say: "I'm not called to be compassionate; that's not my gift. I'm the prophet of the group who calls it like I see it." That's just making excuses and taking Scripture out of context. Surely Jesus embodied all these gifts, and surely he's not lacking in any of them—but when John wrote, *Whoever claims to live in him must live as Jesus did (1 John 2:6)*, he wasn't saying that you and I need to be the jack-of-all-trades (or jill-of-all-trades). You and I must have the character of Christ, but the roles we play in the church are at times radically different. If we want to have the space to navigate criticism well, we have to bury the idea that we are called to do all things well. You're not—and neither am I. You can't—and neither can I.

But why talk about this in a book on criticism? You're supposed to be getting help with criticism, not signing up for more, right?

Remember that we're focused less on responding to our critics and more on identifying the things that make their criticism worse. We're digging in our souls in search of what causes us to be so wrecked by people's critical remarks. To that end, one of the first steps in being able to deal with our critics is to accept the fact that if you and I act like we've been called by God to be a one-person show, we will believe that *everything* matters. And that sets us up for a serious case of "I-can't-take-it-anymore" criticism nightmares.

One indicator that this might be you is how you answer this question: "How are you doing—REALLY?"

If your answer is "I'm slammed" or "I'm tired because I haven't slept in days," this might be you. If you have no margin for any meetings to go long, for a car to break, and for a plan to not run perfectly, then you might want to read this chapter a time or two before moving on. Sure, there are seasons when we all get busy. Christmas is one. If you're a parent, both the beginning and end of the school year qualify. If you're an accountant, then December and April will be stupid busy. I get that.

I don't know about you, but I can live there in this busyness if I don't keep it in check. My default is to take on too much and to do too much, thinking it's a way to show that I love God and love others. However, when I do that, I also have no margin. I'm always tired. I'm running from one thing to the next. And if you send me a nasty email, or tell me my talk could have been better, or try to correct the way I'm leading my staff, I have no space for it. I can't step back and take a walk to ponder it. I can't let it marinate and seek counsel from others who know me better. I'm just slammed, and your criticism becomes the grain of salt that tipped the scale. It was the "last straw," so to speak.

In fact, all criticism has a "last straw" connotation to it when we live our lives on tilt. If it is true that everyone gets criticism, then it is also true that everyone does stuff that will cause those words to be misread, overly weighted, and more wounding than they're worth. If you are already overwhelmed, then any critical comment you receive will be, by default, overwhelming.

So before you sign up to be your own one-person band and single-act show, know this: If you follow that path, then all the criticism that comes your way will be yours alone, too. And when it is, you'll likely not have the space or sanity to deal with it wisely. So from one youth worker, one parent, one spouse, one co-worker to another who genuinely wrestles with this one—join me in cutting yourself some slack, and back away from that to-do list. It's not all yours, and when that thing on the list doesn't happen and someone complains about it, you'll be able to confidently and humbly say, "Well, I'm sorry you feel that way. Sounds like something we need to work on"—and then go to sleep and deal with it another day. Because you won't be so overwhelmed that you can't handle it.

SOME QUESTIONS TO PONDER:

- Which of these five issues from Section One has the most influence on how you respond to criticism? Which tends to create the greatest distortion on your perspective?

    - An identity in what you do instead of who you are

    - The unseen but very real baggage when the thing people criticize is also how you pay the bills

    - The comparison game that you're losing to your imaginary opponents

    - The inability to accept success as a process and admit some failure as inevitable along the way

    - The tendency to live a life of self-dependency at a margin-less pace

- What would you add to this list? What else makes criticism deeply affect you?

- If you've identified a thing or two that tends to rock your soul, how can you respond in healthier ways? What action steps do you need to take in order to make room for criticism so it doesn't destroy you?

- Is there anyone whose criticism you have received recently that you need to rethink (or at least rethink your response to) in light of the new realization that it was actually pretty loaded for you because of one of these reasons? Is it possible that the person offering the criticism might have no idea that you had so much on the line and that they stepped on a minefield without knowing it?

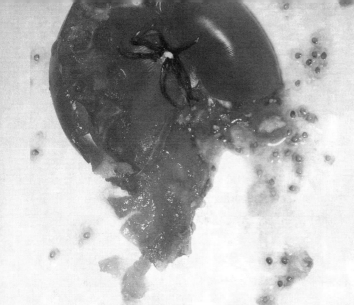

SECTION TWO
LEARNING FROM AND RESPONDING TO YOUR CRITICS

In the spirit of criticism and maybe a little comic relief, we all need to have a plan to deal with the funk that comes our way. For example, as a youth pastor, my house has ended up in a funk due to it being toilet papered a time or two. Students and sometimes even volunteer staff will come by and feel my house needs some decorating at 1 a.m. They'll add strips of white to my cars, spread it around the yard, even occasionally get bold enough to think they can decorate the backyard. A few times they even managed to get inside of my car and my office.

The week before I went off to college, someone toilet papered my house. I didn't catch them. However, they were in such a hurry and left so many nearly full rolls that I put them all in a large trash bag and took them to college. I didn't have to buy a roll my entire first quarter at the University of California at Davis.

Not wanting my quarterly supply of TP to be dropped off in my lawn at night, it didn't take me long to discover that I needed to have a more memorable response to toilet papering and pranks or my house would be the chief target of this activity every Friday night and my life would be a perpetual practical joke. I had a friend who used to say, "I don't get mad. I don't get even. I just get one or two up." I decided that this sounded like a good plan, and I set out to implement it. So I began to pass out some thank you's of my own. I could share a bunch of stories, but here are three quick ones...

The first group I caught toilet papering my house, I chased down the street. I caught one of the kids and hosed them down from top to bottom. Word got around.

Another time a student found a "hide-a-key" in a fake rock by our front door. (Side note: Don't hide your key in a fake rock; it looks like a place someone would hide a key!) He got into my house, took all the cabinet doors off the hinges, sunk the screws in a bag in the bottom of my fish tank, and removed the labels from all my canned goods. My wife was none too happy. A few days later when he left school to go to his car, he found his car in the parking lot on all four tires. However, they had been removed and were now sitting on the rims, which were flat on the ground. Word got around—and I got rid of the hide-a-key and got a dog.

The most historic, however, was the girl who broke into my truck while it was in her driveway and I was having a conversation with her mom inside. She filled my car with various items and spread girl lotion smell everywhere. In response, I secretly asked her mom if she would let me decorate her daughter's room—and I got permission. One day while the girl was at school, I filled her closet with confetti and her room with hundreds of balloons. What I didn't get permission for was the 2-pound trout that I left on newspaper under her bed. About two days later, that got me in a lot of trouble, but it also got me a "Don't mess with Brian" reputation that lasted for years.

While I'm not advocating a retaliation policy for your critics (though I know that sounds fun), I am suggesting that we need a better plan of attack. I'm also not suggesting that you implement my "don't get mad and don't get even—just get one or two up" prank policy on them either, though I've been tempted a time or two myself. Instead, when it comes to criticism, we need to think both practically and theologically about how God can use criticism in our lives and how we can learn to respond to it in healthy ways. So for the next section of this book we'll commence on a journey together to answer the "I've got a critic—now what?" question that is looming.

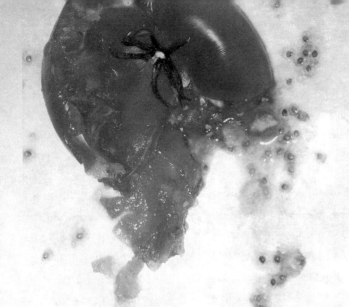

CHAPTER 7

KEEPING THE MAIN THING THE MAIN THING

My grandma used to have this plaque on her wall in her home office that read, "I can only please one God per day. Today is not your day. Tomorrow does not look good either." But mounting it on your wall and living that way in your heart are two very different things. One requires a nail and some wall space; the other requires some theological soul surgery.

Perhaps this is why Paul asks this question to the churches in Galatia: *Am I now trying to win the approval of human beings, or of God? Or am I trying to please people?* Then he answers his own question in the same vein as my grandma's wall plaque with this kicker of a conclusion: *If I were still trying to please people, I would not be a servant of Christ (Galatians 1:10)*. Stew on that for a while. Paul says that if I'm trying to keep people happy instead of primarily being concerned with pleasing God, I'm no longer serving God—now I'm serving people. This can appear immensely confusing because in Paul's writings to the church in Corinth, he famously writes this: *To the weak I became weak, to win the weak. I have become all things to all people so that by all possible means I might save some (1 Corinthians 9:22)*. So evangelism changes it, and I can please people if they are far from God? What?

Then to the church in Rome he writes this: *If it is possible, as far as it depends on you, live at peace with everyone (Romans 12:18)*. This seems ludicrous. Which advice do I follow? Am I supposed to go out of my way to keep people happy, or not? Evidently, in Paul's heart there's a difference between living at *peace* with people and living to *please* people. That might be a fine line, but it's one that the Scriptures call us to dance around—and one that is crucial to a healthy response to criticism.

Before you go rushing off to the leadership ER trauma wing in an effort to fix what's wrong or deal with every fire that comes your way as though they all have equal capacity to burn down your house, let's agree on a few things:

First, our goal is to please God. Period. Let's stack hands and agree that the ancient call of Moses to the people of Israel has not changed for us. *It is the Lord your God you must follow, and him you must revere. Keep his commands and obey him; serve him and hold fast to him (Deuteronomy 13:4).* There is no other name we can substitute for God in there. The voice we are seeking to follow, the leading we want to obey, the criticism we want to heed, the only focus of our lives—it is God alone. Let's remind ourselves that the word *Christian* was not the primary label for the early church. It was *followers of the Way* (see Acts 22:4). They were known as people who followed Jesus and embodied the call to live in the way that Jesus lived (see 1 John 2:6). So all criticism must be filtered through that lens. How is this word moving us to please God? If we can't clearly articulate how this word will move us toward God, then we call it what it is: not from God.

Second, some people are simply unpleaseable. My dictionary says that's not a word. Well, it is evidently unpleaseable, too, because whether my dictionary or anyone else wants to admit it, these people exist and they like to criticize others. A lot.

When I was in college, we called one guy in our church the "spiritual fruit and gift inspector" because he thought he was always right. He also evidently felt God had commissioned him to tell anyone and everyone where they were wrong. If you give $5 on a Sunday to each adult who walks into your church and ask them to use it to perform a random act of kindness as an application to your message, this is the guy who won't think it's awesome. The "unpleaseables" will think it's a waste of money and will send you their $5 back in the offering envelope with a lengthy note telling you why you are not stewarding God's resources well.

If you plan a mission trip to Haiti, they'll tell you to send the money to the Haitian people instead and they'll say that you could feed more kids with the money you'll be wasting on airfare. If you give them small group curriculum to teach, they'll tell you it doesn't fit their group. If you let them write their own curriculum, they'll tell you that you give them no support. I wish I were kidding. But before you go bending over backward to help some of your critics be happy, accept the fact that you can't bend far enough. And in the attempt to please God, some people will choose to never be on his side and they'll complain to God about it, too.

First Thessalonians 1 begins with a greeting from Paul, Silas, and Timothy, who were putting their heads together to send a letter to the church of the Thessalonians. They reminded this group of believers, like the churches in Galatia, that they should not try to please them, but God: *On the contrary, we speak as those approved by God to be entrusted with the gospel. We are not trying to please people but God, who tests our hearts (1 Thessalonians 2:4).* It's worth noting *why* Scripture says they had the confidence to tell this to the church. The foundation of their confidence wasn't in their arrogance or the idea that they were better than their critics. It was not an instruction to Christ-followers that they should have been trying to please Paul or the Apostles or anyone else. Instead it was a call for all of them to foundationally identify themselves not as the critical ones but as ones who are "approved by God."

The Apostle John reminds us that we need to look to our identity as "children of God" often. He writes this: *See what great love the Father has lavished on us, that we should be called children of God! And that is what we are! (1 John 3:1).* This is a profound truth we must remember when dealing with criticism. I'm not earning anything by pleasing people. What more can I gain beyond being a child of God? Perhaps this is at the core of the question Jesus asks of his disciples: *"What good is it for someone to gain the whole world, yet forfeit their soul?" (Mark 8:36).* Let's vow to not be the ones who win the approval of people at the expense of the approval of God. What a horrible exchange.

Third, leaders tend to be their own worst critics. I think one of the reasons many of us struggle with discouragement and depression (more on that in the next chapter) is because we think more critically than others, especially of ourselves. Leaders know not only what went right at a given event, but also what went wrong. You know what was on the schedule that didn't happen. You know where the plan was just off or where the attendance was just shy of your goal.

My wife still remembers that the custom-printed dessert napkins from our wedding 19 years ago never made it to the cake table. Not one person at the wedding missed them. Not one person complained about them. But my wife had them custom made, planned to have them out, gave them to the caterer, and then much to her dismay took boxes of them home to be used at our dinner table for a year. Not exactly the plan she had in mind.

Sometimes this pleasing-God thing needs to be applied to the person in the mirror, too. It's not just the voice of your critics through emails and phone calls and confronting faces that often are not from God. It also can be the voice in your head that won't shut up, the one that sees you as a failure and constantly rips into you.

Personally, I get this. I love building stuff. I love planning and dreaming, and I can tell you what something could be and should be. I also can tell you where everything is just off. I know where the subtle flaws are, where a font was blurry or just off-center in a flier. I notice the light strand in the ceiling of our high school room that's out. I know when a table is not level. I know where my talk hits home and where I think I rushed. I know too much—and if I'm not careful, I can start living to please the critic in me instead of following the leading of the Holy Spirit in my life.

During the 2012 Simply Youth Ministry Conference in Louisville, Kentucky, I heard Jon Acuff talk about what he called "critic's math." He said that when he would look at the book reviews he was getting on Amazon, he seemed to care so much more about the negative ones than the positive ones. This totally resonated with me. It seems that my critics always have a louder voice than my proponents all the time. Critic's math, Acuff said, goes like this:

1 Insult + 1,000 Compliments = 1 Insult

Wait—what? Yup. That's how it works. You can get five thanks from students after a trip, social media lights up with pictures of them having the time of their life, and then one parent sends you a note telling you their daughter felt judged and doesn't want to come back—and you're done. If you're like most of us, all you can hear is the one negative comment. It's like that annoying song you heard on your way to work that you can't get out of your head all day.

Our last Christmas party for our high school students was a HUGE success. We exceeded our numbers, we laughed, the room looked amazing, students invited their friends. The catered food was good, the talent was off the charts, the pictures were worth 10,000 words. Seriously, it was so good. And compared to the year before—when I was wondering why we even did this anymore and if I should quit my job and go do something I was remotely good at—I was on cloud nine.

Then two days later, my phone was being lit up by the caterer. I couldn't figure out why until I met with the manager and discovered that one of his employees was accused of stealing several hundred dollars from them that night. Unfortunately, the employee in question was my main contact—and he's a friend of mine. It was the second year in a row that my friend catered our food, and I thought it was so good. I was devastated because this accusation was going to cost him his job. He had a wife and kids, a critical surgery on the horizon, and it was just days before Christmas. I was floored.

As I shared the news with our lead pastor, who is also friends with this man, he stopped me and said, "Hey, don't let this shake you. You had an amazing event and God was at work, and I don't want this to be the thing you hold on to. You had no control over his actions." Those are the words of someone who has been there and done that. He knows that leaders tend to hold on to criticism and let it become our banner instead of holding on to the good stuff. More importantly, like Paul and Timothy and Silas reminded the Thessalonian church, it is about our identity in Jesus. I'm not tying to please students or parents or my pastor or my boss or the caterer from a place of neutrality. I'm called to do all of this from my position as a child of God, and therein lies a HUGE truth that deserves more than just a head-nod agreement.

We need to keep the main thing the main thing. And for you and me, the main thing is the only one that truly matters. It is God and God alone who will test our hearts, and ultimately peace comes from God, not from a criticism-free life. God's math is a lot like Acuff's critic's math—but with a twist. It goes like this:

1 God Approval + 1,000 Criticisms = 1 God Approval

Think about it. Remember the promise of Romans 8: *What, then, shall we say in response to these things? If God is for us, who can be against us? (Romans 8:31).* BAM! If God is for you, who cares what your critics say—even that pesky voice in your own head? So here's the only question I really need to ask when criticism comes: "Is God in this?" In other words, "If I move in the direction this critical comment wants me to, will I be moving closer to God or further from him?" The answer is not always a simple yes or no, but nonetheless that's the main thing. That's the goal we all need to remember as the foundation for our responses to those who are critical of us.

One way that I've sought to silence the voice of critic's math is to get in the habit of holding on to my positive and encouraging notes. I'll admit that they don't come so often that I have a huge pile of them, but over the years they've begun to accumulate. I print emails and put them in a box. I keep cards I get. I even print screenshots from Facebook® and capture text messages sometimes. It's like I'm on a hungry search for an encouraging word.

Every once in a while, I take the time to flip though them. There are stories from a talk I gave in college. "Thank you" notes from weddings I performed. Testimonies of a student who was so thankful for a talk I gave or a conversation we had. That box has notes from mentors, family members, and former students—and even an apology or two. Taking the time to flip through it a couple of times a year reminds me that my life is not foundationally made up of my critics' negative comments. I can give credence to other voices, too. They should not be outshouted by the ones that are less happy with me.

One more parting thought here before we move on. Let's not forget this:

No one, not even Jesus, has ever been free of critics.

In fact, people rejected him, followers betrayed him, and plenty thought the call was too tough so they straight-up walked away from him. So when your critics pile up and you feel lonely and believe you're the only person in the world who experiences this, go ahead and confidently repeat this call: "The Holy Spirit is with me. I'm adopted through Jesus, and as a dearly loved child, I will follow God's example" (see Ephesians 1:5 and 5:1). Go ahead and go forward, knowing that God is with you. Seek to please God and God alone, and the critics can fade into the background where they belong in the first place.

SOME QUESTIONS TO PONDER:

- Who in your life do you need the permission to label *unpleasable*? How does this admission change things? What does it release you from? What has God called you to do regardless of your ability or inability to please them?

- When someone says, "I'm my own worst critic," does that resonate with you? Why or why not? How does pleasing God affect the way you respond to your own voice of self-criticism?

- Reflect on "critic's math" vs. "God's math." How do these equations play out in your own life? Who tends to have the greatest voice in your life, and what changes are needed to the weight you give certain voices over others?

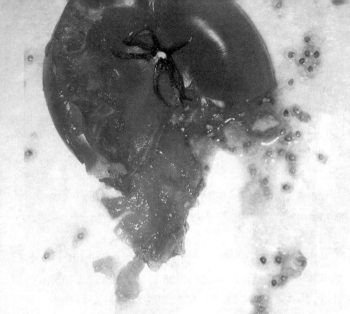

CHAPTER 8
GETTING
ANOTHER
VANTAGE
POINT

My parents tried everything to find the burning smell. First they thought the old VCR/DVD player must be dying—so they got rid of it. Then they replaced the TV, thinking that any day it was going to catch the whole house on fire. But the smell persisted, so they unplugged everything in the family room in search of the one thing that was going to self-destruct any day—but they still could not identify the source. Finally, in a moment of desperation and to get a professional opinion, they broke down and called the fire department.

A fire engine showed up, and four firefighters went in search of the smell with special smoke detectors. They said it smelled kind of like something was burning. No smoke. Just a burnt smell, and faint at that. But they couldn't find the source. Finally, one firefighter got down on all fours and smelled the floor. He said, "I think it's your carpet." "Are you serious?" my mom asked. "Yeah," he said. "I think for some reason, this big rug smells burnt." So then all the firefighters and my parents sniffed the floor like a pack of dogs in search of an intruder and confirmed that yup, it wasn't a dying electronic item or a faulty wire—it was a terminally ill floor rug. (I know. I wish I had a picture of that scene.) But the moral of the story is this: There are times in life when you simply can't get to the truth on your own and you need another perspective.

If you've ever taken your car to a mechanic and said, "Um, I'm not sure where, but back there somewhere, something is making a lot of noise," then you know what I mean. If you've ever asked a friend to help you sort out a problem you're having with your parents, then you get it. If you've ever been to a counselor, or asked for a second opinion on a big purchase, or coached anyone in any sport, then you know that to make the right call on some things, they simply can't be seen from just one angle. This is particularly true when it comes to dealing with criticism. To wisely respond to and learn from our critics, we need another vantage point. Here are some reasons why:

WE ALL NEED ANOTHER VANTAGE POINT TO SEE OURSELVES CLEARLY

It's risky to respond to critics from our own vantage point. If we can't figure out simple things such as broken cars and the source of a funky smell without help, then surely we should not depend on just our own eyes and ears to sort through the emotionally charged power of critical comments. If you've ever responded to an email or social media comment in anger, then you probably have experienced the pain of what happens when we don't ask others to read it first. If you've ever talked yourself into depression because you made a false assumption that someone was angry with you, only to discover that you'd misread their comments the whole time, then you know why another vantage point is not an optional ideal. It is a mandatory step for health. Listen to the collective wisdom of Proverbs:

> *Do not be wise in your own eyes; fear the Lord and shun evil (Proverbs 3:7).*

> *There is a way that appears to be right, but in the end it leads to death (Proverbs 16:25).*

> *Do you see a person wise in their own eyes? There is more hope for a fool than for them (Proverbs 26:12).*

> *Let someone else praise you, and not your own mouth; an outsider, and not your own lips (Proverbs 27:2).*

We're in a dangerous place when we think the mirror reflects the whole truth. It does not, and the book of Proverbs warns us to not fall into this trap. To respond wisely, we need to filter any significant criticism or critical adjustment through the eyes and ears of a community of Christ-followers. So before you respond too quickly, before you rethink your whole ministry, before you die on that hill, and before you quit your job—get advice from a different vantage point of some trusted mentors.

If you flash back to the scenario with "John" and the season of ministry when I tried to quit, you'll remember that I found myself neck-deep in criticism and unable to navigate it. I couldn't sleep. I couldn't eat. I couldn't stop crying. I was a mess. It was the eyes of two pastors in particular that helped me sort through it all. Without them, I promise you that I would have handled it differently, and without them, I would not be who I am today. I desperately needed another vantage point because criticism had me pinned down, unable to get up and look around clearly.

Years later, my wife and I felt God was calling us to move out of our ministry context and to seek another, and it was clear that this was going to be no small move. We had two young boys at the time, and my wife was pregnant with our third, so it was going to impact our family and where we raised our kids. I was serving in the ministry where I had cut my teeth, so it was going to be a ministry transition that I'd never done before. Our friends and family all lived in the area, so it was going to impact our social life and ease of support. All of this was staring us in the face when we began to consider that God might be calling us somewhere else.

So I called up mentors and asked for advice. One person gave me a list of questions to ask churches. I submitted a budget to my parents for a set of wise eyes in regards to salary needs. I asked men I respected if they thought I was disobeying God by not jumping right away and taking a risk of faith and quitting my job, even though we didn't have a deep savings account to fall back on. I also knew things weren't all bad and that some people would not be happy with my decision. I anticipated some criticism would come my way. I knew I'd be affecting families and our church and our community that we'd grown to love, so as I stepped into this sea of uncertainty, I did so with the support and wisdom of a team.

During another season of life, when Shannon and I felt like the Lord was leading us to adopt 5-year-old twins from Uganda, we went searching for counsel. I grabbed every man I respected and took them out for a LONG cup of coffee. I shared my fears, my hopes, my dreams. I reflected what I was thinking and praying, and asked for advice. I asked them for encouragement and correction, and I got both. In the end, some of it was at odds with advice from other mentors in the same circle. So Shannon and I had to put it all in a bowl and offer it up to God and jump out in faith as we adopted Becky and Billy into our family, even in the midst of criticism from some people who thought that it was not wise. In the end, we believe it was God's plan for us, but it obviously created a tremendous domino effect on every area of our life, ministry, and family. This was not the kind of thing you sort through on your own.

Since that time, I've had several friends use a "Quaker Clearness Committee"[5] to help them reflect on a major life decision or even to respond to a critic. A clearness committee can be assembled through a variety of methods and means, but essentially it's a group of friends that gather around someone who is facing a critical decision or crisis and is looking for wisdom or discernment on a leading they think might be from God. In the case of criticism, it is a great way to try to sort through what you've been thinking with a group of people you love and respect. According to the official page of the Quaker Friends General Conference[6], here are four of the many things that a good clearness committee will do for you:

- Listen tenderly to the questions and concerns you have

- Ask you careful, open-ended questions to help define what you are feeling called to do

- Reflect back what they have heard

- Make recommendations based on what they've heard

It's not a three-day event. It's more like a long dinner. If you want, I'm sure the same method could be applied to a group of four friends meeting over coffee and agreeing to give their undivided focus to one member's hurting soul. When you're in a season of uncertainty and your critics are squawking, this is something you should seriously consider doing. But regardless of what method you choose, being in the midst of criticism is no time to stand alone; it is a time to begin the process toward health with another vantage point. We need people to speak truth and help us sort through the good, the bad, and the ugly of our lives.

WE ALL NEED ANOTHER VANTAGE POINT TO BECOME WHO GOD HAS FULLY MADE US TO BE

All of those verses in Proverbs are also a warning to those who think they can become all that God has called them to be without the input of others. It's like an Olympic athlete thinking they can become the best in the world without a coach.

Not. Gonna. Happen.

When was the last time you heard about an athlete without a coach? Even professional golfers ask for advice and criticism from their caddies about how the game should be played. All professional athletes—yes, ALL professional athletes—have coaches. Yet have you ever noticed that, at least when we're talking about coaches for professional adult athletes, all the athletes can outplay their coaches? If this were not true, the coach would still be the quarterback, or the goalie, or the 100-meter sprinter.

Every time I watch the Olympics I find this to be fascinating. The very best in the world are being coached by the "not the very best in the world." In fact, most times the coach *never* was the best in the world at what they are coaching! So it's not a "better than" viewpoint a coach is offering; it's simply wisdom and insight from a perspective the athletes cannot get on their own. World-class athletes know that if they want to improve their performance, they need someone who can see what they cannot see for one reason or another. Those who don't seek coaching or assistance often find themselves in one of these scenarios: (1) They hit a plateau caused by their own limitations or (2) they become self-righteous and arrogant, believing they are self-made and therefore need no one. Both are bad. Both are a loss.

One of my own personal aha's in this area came from a time when I was teaching in the main service in my first church. I was telling a story to illustrate a point. To be honest, I don't even remember what text or point I was illustrating. I only recall that I'd noticed earlier that week, while preparing my sermon, that someone had taken a Lamborghini to the local gas station for repairs. Perhaps the man owned the station or perhaps the mechanic owned the car, but as I drove by, I found it incredibly odd. There was a $250,000 car up on hydraulic lifts next to a $5,000 truck getting an oil change in a corner gas station.

So in my message, I was describing this and how silly it was and that I thought how if you had the money to own a Lamborghini, you should also have the money to have it fixed right. Whatever my point was, I was making fun of the anonymous car owner in order to illustrate this idea. Maybe one reason that I don't remember much about the story is because of what happened next. After the sermon, one of the elders gently pulled me aside and put his arm around me. He said, "Thanks for your sermon today, Brian. But I just wanted you to know that the owner of that Lamborghini is a friend of mine—and he was here today." I looked at him with embarrassment and shock, and then he paused—and in a calm, humble, and sincere tone he said, "No, he wasn't and I don't know him. But he could have been." I looked back and said, "Thank you. Point well made. I heard you."

I didn't need anything more. I knew that his point was right and that I needed to consider the cost of my sarcasm and decide if the risk was worth it in the future. He actually was trying to help me become God's best. This kind of correction is not the stuff I can muster up. It must come from an outside source. He wasn't trying to destroy me. I needed another vantage point to help me.

WE ALL NEED ANOTHER VANTAGE POINT TO SEE OTHERS MORE CLEARLY

Sometimes I don't see myself well. Sometimes I don't see God's best well. Other times, I can't read people very well. When the issue is criticism, about 90 percent of the time I'm not going to read my critic well or at least not from an unbiased vantage point.

Have you ever had a few friends with a triangulated relationship through you? You know, the one where you get along with Sally and with Bob just fine, but Bob and Sally don't get along at all. I have several of those relationships, and in each of them, it's not that I'm some super friend— it's just that I see something in each person that they can't see in each other.

In the famous story of Mary and Martha (Luke 10:38-42), Jesus was the triangulated one. He loved both Mary and Martha, but at that moment Martha was not a fan of Mary. According to Martha, Mary was sitting around while she was busting her chops in the kitchen. In the end, Jesus confronted Mary and told her that she was in the wrong in this situation. Then the story just stops. We don't know if Mary stomped out. We don't know if she put down her things and started to listen to Jesus. Or maybe she burnt the meal and they all went out to dinner and she said, "See, I told you someone should've been in the kitchen." Nothing. What we do know is that Martha didn't understand Mary, and Mary presumably was thinking, "What is she doing in there? Doesn't she know Jesus is here and he doesn't care about the table setting?" They were reading each other wrong, and it took another view to sort it out.

Paul was in this same situation with some Jews over the issue of whether Gentile converts had to be circumcised. He said no. Some Jews said yes. They didn't understand each other, so to get the answer, they went to Jerusalem to meet with the apostles and the elders there and to make a sound decision based on their collective wisdom (Acts 15). They needed another vantage point to understand one another and to make a God-honoring decision.

I can't even begin to count the number of times when someone in my life has come alongside me to help me read someone else. Many times I've sought out the advice of a trusted member of our team or staff to help me understand someone else on the team. I've asked trusted friends for counsel in regards to my wife and kids. I've sought advice to understand the motives of volunteers and paid staff. I've brought complaints from one congregation member to my pastoral team to get their collective wisdom on how to respond. One time I wasn't clicking with a guy I had hired, so I went to his old boss and said, "I think I'm missing something. I know you guys got along fabulously, which is why we hired him in the first place. Can you tell me what I'm missing?" I needed a different vantage point in each of these situations because from where I was sitting, I was in a funk with someone and couldn't sort it out on my own.

The next time your critics come calling, before you crawl into a corner or start making changes or pick up a stick and start swinging, run it by someone you respect who has a different vantage point. You'll be so glad you did, and I promise that you'll save yourself and even your critics from a world of unnecessary hurt.

SOME QUESTIONS TO PONDER:

- Who are the people that you could or do go to for another wise vantage point in your life?

- What are some examples of people who have given you criticism or correction along the way that, looking back on it, you now see offered wisdom from a vantage point you could not personally see at the time?

- Have you ever assembled your own "Quaker Clearness Committee"? If you have, what was that like for you? If you have not, is there a situation you're in that this could help with? Who do you need to ask to be part of that group?

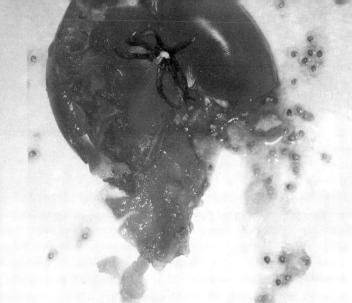

CHAPTER 9

DISCOURAGEMENT DOESN'T COME FROM GOD

After a Sunday morning service about three years into ministry, I was handed a huge stack of envelopes with note cards all rubber banded together. Why? Well, somewhere in the world of Christendom, someone had evidently decided that it was Pastor Appreciation Day. For me, this day was akin to National Secretary's Day (or Administrative Professionals Day, as some people now call it). It's a nice idea, but for most people, it is forgotten, is ignored, or passes us by unnoticed until someone else points it out. So I rarely paid attention and never had my expectations very high.

On Pastor Appreciation Day, occasionally some old lady would stick a note and a box of candy in my mailbox at work. A couple of longtime church families might buy a note card from the local Christian bookstore and sign it. Sometimes there'd be a gift card inside, too. But that was the normal routine for this weekend. Honestly, I didn't even know it was that Sunday, and I'm pretty sure my students would not have either if one of my volunteers hadn't told them. Evidently, while I was doing various things throughout the morning, he was wooing students into a back room and giving them the opportunity to write "thank you" notes.

Then at the end of our youth group hour, much to my surprise he said our morning was not done. He walked up front and thanked me for my investment as a pastor. He said how much he loved working with me, expressed how appreciative all my students were, and then handed me that pile of note cards. The group prayed over me, and I was totally surprised and a little taken aback. I thanked him and told my students that I would be sure to read them all when I got home. So that's what I did.

After church I went home and brewed a cup of java. Then I sat down in my recliner to soak up some encouragement. Eventually, about one-third of the way into my stack, I picked up a note with bubble handwriting on the outside that read "thanks" and over the "a" was a great big heart. It looked like a girl had written it, and inside I expected to find the words, "Don't change. Stay cool. See you next Sunday. Ha Ha." as if it were a high school yearbook.

However, inside was a very different story. It was a nice note card with a picture of a horse on the front, but then the contents were written in a handwriting that was radically different from whoever wrote the words on the envelope, with a teeny-tiny font so as to get an essay into the small blank-card space. Inside, this is what it said:

Dear Brian,

The following is but a small portion of the many things we appreciate in you.

We appreciate that religion is your job

We appreciate your vague guidance

We appreciate the fact that you regularly compromise your integrity by buckling under the stark thumbs of the church elders despite your own personal convictions

We appreciate your perseverance, in light of many failed attempts to reform your insubordinate adult leader and student leader groups

We appreciate your contributing to the problem of hubris and self-esteem (or lack thereof) by constantly stressing the so-called importance of things like physical appearance and association (ie: a "Christian Image" as if there was such a thing)

We appreciate your complete bias and favoritism towards students and staff, causing a select few to rise to the top while the mass majority

*of your little minions remain at the bottom of your popularity/power
spectrum only to be overlooked and taken for granted*

*We appreciate your refusal to write new material, enabling us to reuse
notes from previous "messages"*

*We appreciate the fact that you are no better than any of us sheep, and
that your knowledge does not succeed any of ours*

Thanks For Nothing.

That was it. It wasn't signed. It was an anonymous note that quickly
angered me. I immediately was on the defensive and wrote my own
retaliation note as I read it, declaring line by line that it was a total lie.
The part that bugged me the most was the accusation that I'd reused
old messages. *What?* I'd intentionally written every message fresh from
scratch, and the assertion that I had not—well, it made me want to take
someone to court and prove it!

Then I read it again and again and again. I didn't re-read any of the
others. None of the good ones were anonymous, so I pondered who
wrote this. I started making my list of people, analyzing handwriting,
searching for clues—anything. In fact, in the spirit of Jon Acuff's critic's
math, I have no idea what any of the rest of the stack of letters said.
This one criticism plus a stack of encouragement notes had amounted to
one all-encompassing critical stack of notes. This happened before I had
started my encouragement note file box, so sadly, it is the only one that I
saved and still have from that stack.

In nearly 20 years of youth ministry, I've had my share of critical notes
and emails, but none have been as cutting, specific, and belligerent as
this one. I once had a parent write me a three-page letter about why I
should never use the word *butt*, "butt" that was clearly stupid (ha ha,

pun intended). I gave it to my lead pastor, and we read it together and laughed. I'm pretty sure I used that word more creatively after that day, inserting it into sentences during staff meetings just to get a laugh. However, this particular note could not be laughed off like that. It had found a sore spot somewhere in my soul and latched on, and I was too afraid to share it with anyone.

I don't know if you've ever received your own version of that note, but if you've been following Jesus for any length of time in any area of life, you've surely had days when you were deeply discouraged. I've had days when marriage was just too hard, parenting five kids was a mountain too high, life had too high an expectation, and my job seemed pointless. On those days, I plain and simple have wanted to quit.

When those days come, when criticism that cuts deep arrives on your doorstep or gets sent to your inbox, you'll need something besides this chapter to keep you going. You'll need a deep, deep truth. So here are just three truths I hope you truly hold on to.

YOU'RE NOT ALONE

First, you're not alone in your discouragement. You're not the first, and you won't be the last person to be wrecked by it and want to quit. Your friends could testify to this. But for written proof, the Bible is full of examples of people who made a big impact despite criticism:

- **Moses** spent 40 years wandering the desert with millions of complaining people. He had moments of intimacy with God followed by his people worshipping golden calves. He had plenty of days when he asked God, "Why? Seriously, what is going on?"

- **Jeremiah**, in a moment of frustration after having been "ridiculed all day long" for years on end, said to God, "You deceived me."

I'm pretty positive those were a bunch of bad days in his world (Jeremiah 20:7).

- **Solomon** wrote an entire book of the Bible in which he repeats the word *meaningless* as the summation of his experience over and over again. As he looked back at all he'd spent his life doing and building, he concluded that he could have spent his time in better ways. Discouragement is an understatement.

- There's **Peter**. Read his life story. It's like a rollercoaster of the good, the bad, and the discouraged. He hit some home runs and then committed some huge blunders that cost the game in the span of just a few Bible verses. He totally understood this discouragement thing.

- **Paul** was persecuting the very people of God to the death. Then Jesus confronted him on a road, and Paul ended up blind. That was just one of many not-so-uplifting days in his world.

- **Jesus** himself was betrayed by close friends, abandoned by his followers, discouraged by the lack of belief, and even cried out to the Father in desperation as he was forsaken and bore the sins of the world on the cross. He experienced more of the weight of discouragement in three years than any of us can fully understand.

But in terms of the biblical account, perhaps our best example is **David**. As we read the psalms, he gives us a window into the been-there-done-that piece of his soul. As one example, let's consider Psalm 6.

Lord, do not rebuke me in your anger or discipline me in your wrath. Have mercy on me, Lord, for I am faint; heal me, Lord, for my bones are in agony. My soul is in deep anguish. How long, Lord, how long? Turn, Lord, and deliver me; save me because of your unfailing love. Among the dead no one proclaims your name. Who praises you from the grave? I am

*worn out from my groaning. All night long I flood my bed with weeping
and drench my couch with tears. My eyes grow weak with sorrow; they
fail because of all my foes. Away from me, all you who do evil, for
the Lord has heard my weeping. The Lord has heard my cry for mercy;
the Lord accepts my prayer. All my enemies will be overwhelmed with
shame and anguish; they will turn back and suddenly be put to shame
(Psalm 6:1-10).*

Do you hear the words of a man with deep hurt and discouragement in
his bones? All night long he's been crying. His soul is in deep anguish.
His bones are in agony. He is faint. Seriously, it would show up on a
clinical discouragement test. You're not alone in this feeling.

THIS, TOO, SHALL PASS

Notice this question David asks in that psalm: *"How long, Lord, how
long?"* Inherent in the question is an awareness that surely this won't
last for forever. Every time I find myself deeply discouraged *"because of
all my foes,"* the light at the end of the tunnel grows dark and I quickly
feel hopeless. I'm not great at hiding it, especially if I'm tired, stressed,
worried, or already overwhelmed with the demands of life when the
discouragement comes. In those cases, people can read me pretty easily,
and I begin to wonder if I'll ever have a better day.

But that's not the testimony of my bigger story. Like a storm that ruins
homes and rips down power lines, eventually it passes. Discouragement
is not a life sentence; it is a season that will come and go, and in my
experience, it is often tied to seasons of criticism.

One of my deepest discouragements as a youth pastor is the come-and-
go roller coaster of relationships. I have students who I have done some
life with—including some I have experienced truly great life with—but
who then eventually just walked away. I could give you a long list of
these stories, but let's use just one example. I'll call her "Jill."

She was in my youth ministry for three years. She served on our student leadership team and hosted our services. She went to camps and retreats. She was in a small group. She was a joy to do ministry with and someone I looked forward to seeing. I cried with her and laughed with her on too many occasions to count. But then one summer day before her senior year, a switch flipped and almost overnight Jill was gone. Her family that she'd been praying God would finally restore instead fell apart for the last time, and her parents divorced. And when they did, she divorced herself from God. Done. Finished.

For six weeks I bugged and texted and messaged her saying, "Let's talk." I dropped by her house. Nothing worked. I considered her a good friend, and some of my best stories of her high school years came from our memories together. But they were no more. And honestly, it tore me up. Regardless of whose fault it was or what was in or out of my control, the bottom line is that I lost another student as a friend to do life with Jesus with. To this day, I regularly drop in on Jill's Facebook page and pray, but that's as close as I get.

Then I heard that a few weeks ago she decided to "check out the college group" again. And I was reminded that it's not done. Sometimes relationships take years to heal, but I don't have to carry discouragement every day. I have some close friends whose son was in our youth ministry and who has been traveling on his own version of "a prodigal journey" the last several years. I have others who thank me every time they see me for the influence our ministry had on their home. It's almost like discouragement is seasonal.

Some days, discouragement hangs around like a lead balloon. Other days, the wind comes and it is transformed and God lifts it. Regardless of what day it is, don't let discouragement become your identity. Remember that we cannot please people and it's not our call. I won't tell you that discouragement is not a real emotion, but I will remind you that it's not your identity. This, too, shall pass.

DISCOURAGEMENT IS NOT FROM THE LORD

Perhaps the greatest word of encouragement I could give you is this: The very real feeling you have of discouragement from this criticism you're enduring is NOT from the Lord. No, I'm not saying God can't use it. I'm not saying that God will keep you from ever being discouraged or that criticism won't come. I'm just saying that discouragement is never wrapped up in a nice box that reads "To _____ (insert your name)," from "God." Need proof? OK: Six times in the Old Testament we are told that because of the presence of God around us, we should not be discouraged. Interestingly enough, many of these quotes come in the context of a battle, which is exactly what criticism feels like: a battle in your soul. Here they are:

> "The Lord himself goes before you and will be with you; he will never leave you nor forsake you. Do not be afraid; do not be discouraged" (Deuteronomy 31:8).

> "See, the Lord your God has given you the land. Go up and take possession of it as the Lord, the God of your ancestors, told you. Do not be afraid; do not be discouraged" (Deuteronomy 1:21).

> "Have I not commanded you? Be strong and courageous. Do not be afraid; do not be discouraged, for the Lord your God will be with you wherever you go" (Joshua 1:9).

> Then the Lord said to Joshua, "Do not be afraid; do not be discouraged" (Joshua 8:1).

> Joshua said to them, "Do not be afraid; do not be discouraged. Be strong and courageous. This is what the Lord will do to all the enemies you are going to fight" (Joshua 10:25).

"You will not have to fight this battle. Take up your positions; stand firm and see the deliverance the Lord will give you, Judah and Jerusalem. Do not be afraid; do not be discouraged. Go out to face them tomorrow, and the Lord will be with you" (2 Chronicles 20:17).

Go ahead. Read this aloud: Discouragement is NOT from God. Seriously, say it out loud. Yes, even right there in Starbucks®. It's good news, and maybe someone else besides you needs to hear it, too! Seriously, it's time to own this thing!

As I've pondered this and compared it with the way I often feel, I've also been reminded of the fruit God says his Spirit brings us. Notice the list: *But the fruit of the Spirit is love, joy, peace, forbearance, kindness, goodness, faithfulness, gentleness and self-control. Against such things there is no law (Galatians 5:22-23).* Now notice what's not on the list. Discouragement didn't make the cut. That is because it's not a fruit of the Spirit and it's NOT from the Lord. Criticism or correction can come from God. But the discouragement that we attach to it—that's the devil riding shotgun. He's like the mold attached to a perfectly good block of cheese. Just cut it off and move on. The whole batch isn't bad, but that section is not good.

I once heard a story about Mother Teresa. I had gone to the Promise Keepers pastors gathering in Atlanta in 1996[7] where almost 40,000 pastors gathered for a national time of prayer and encouragement. It was pretty amazing, and in the days leading up to it, they held a gathering for youth pastors. During it, this one gal was talking about serving in Calcutta, India, and getting a chance to meet Mother Teresa. As she interacted with the group, her only question was this: "Did you find joy in your serving?" Then she said, "If you didn't do it with joy, it didn't count." For Mother Teresa, the fruit of joy was an indicator of the presence of the Holy Spirit. Incidentally, I think joy is the first thing to go when discouragement sets in.

So let's get really practical for a minute and summarize our conclusions so far. You have a source of discouragement from a critic. Maybe it's your boss. Maybe it's a family member or a peer or simply a voice in your head. Or maybe it's some combination of those. What should you do?

First, do not let it become your identity, because you're a child of God and not merely a receiver of criticism. Second, gather some people who can help you think straight on this, because you're deep in this thing and it's hard to see clearly from your vantage point. Third, separate the wheat from the chaff. Maybe you can learn something from a wheat kernel of truth that's in the criticism, but the discouragement that came with it is the chaff and is not from God. Declare it as such. Discouragement is NOT from God.

SOME QUESTIONS TO PONDER:

- Of the long list of biblical characters who endured some criticism along the road of following God, who do you find the most connection with? Why? When you're discouraged, which biblical character gives you hope and the reminder that you're not alone in this feeling? In what ways are you like them?

- When was the last time you were seriously discouraged? What brought it on? What did the voice in your head say to you? What did others say? Where did you go for help?

- On a scale of 1 to 10 (1 being not at all and 10 being desperately needed), how important is the reminder that "Discouragement does not come from God" in your life right now? If discouragement does not come from God, but from the devil, where has the devil managed to plant the seed of discouragement in your life? What needs to be done to uproot it in and around you?

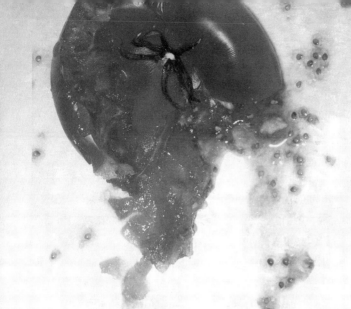

CHAPTER 10
COMMUNICATION, COMMUNICATION, COMMUNICATION

I was in my office when I got one of those messages. "Hey, can we meet to talk?" You know what your brain does with those, right? Didn't you immediately go with me to the "I did something wrong" assumption? Because of this, I have learned to reply and ask for more details, so I did. I said, "Sure" and asked, "Anything specific you'd like to talk about?" I got this reply: "Yes, but I'd rather not say. Can we talk face-to-face?" I hate that response. Not because I wouldn't rather talk face-to-face, but because of the anonymity of the meeting subject. Now my brain went even deeper into thinking, "Oh my, now I know I'm in trouble." So I set up the meeting, and it started as I expected.

Let's call the mom "Sharon" and her daughter "Kathy." I was meeting just with Sharon, but it turns out she wanted to talk about Kathy, who was in high school. Sharon was having some trouble with her, and some of it was related to youth group. I was already on my heels because of my assumptions in setting up the meeting, but for about 10 minutes she expressed how her daughter was disconnected from friends and having a hard time at school and in youth group. She was concerned about her behavior. She talked about cliques in our youth group and how Kathy was having trouble breaking in.

Finally I interrupted her to offer at least a word of defense. As I began explaining that her daughter wasn't exactly exerting much energy in our ministry and then offered some corrections of my own, Sharon burst into tears. I couldn't figure out what I had said or what to do, so I just sat there as she collected herself. Then, through tears she said to me, "I know all of that. I just wanted you to listen. I needed someone to hear me out and give me some help. I don't know what to do with Kathy right now, and I can't take it anymore."

I felt 2 feet tall. No offense to 2-foot-tall people, but I could have crawled under a toddler door at that moment. I spent the next hour trying to undo my false assumptions and offer some suggestions that might help. I apologized. I learned some lessons—not the least of which is that communication is rarely clear and before I go responding to what I think is being labeled my fault, I should at least make sure my perceived critics and I are talking about the same thing.

In fact, I think we could boil down the source of most conflict—and the criticism that is attached to it—to bad communication. Letters are misread by inserting a tone of voice that is not there. Words mean different things to different people. Comments are taken out of context. Opportunities for clarification are missing. Body language is absent. Assumptions of what was said and meant are all over the place. "He said, she said" trains of bad information are abundant, and the real story is all too easily lost in bad communication.

Toastmasters is a group similar to a speechwriters club or a speakers club. I've never been a part of it, but I had a mentor in college who was once a member of it. He said that one of their exercises that helps people understand how communication can get confusing is to put different emphases on different words in the following sentence: "I didn't say you were stupid." So they have participants say it six different times, changing the emphasis to each word in the sentence to change the meaning.

I didn't say you were stupid… he did.

I **didn't** say you were stupid… I definitely did not.

I didn't **say** you were stupid… I only implied it.

I didn't say **you** were stupid… I said she was stupid.

I didn't say you **were** stupid… I said you are stupid.

I didn't say you were **stupid**… I said you were stupendous.

Think about that in terms of written language. When we get an "irate" email, how much of that anger comes from the way we are reading it? If you want to meet and won't tell me why, I assume I'm in trouble. Or if your words are in **bold**, I assume that your tone got angry and probably louder. We have no way of verifying emphasis and tone, so we assume that if the email is in ALL CAPS, THE PERSON IS YELLING AT US. But that's not always true.

I once heard Max Lucado read the questions that God asks of Job near the end of that book (see Job 38–39), and it blew me away because I've always read them with a "let me put your whining self into place" tone of voice as God billows questions from heaven. But Lucado read them with an honest and humble tone, as if God was lovingly reminding Job that he didn't know all that God knows. It was astonishing how my response to the words changed, based on how Lucado read them.

So here are a few basic rules I employ with criticism:

1. Don't assume you understood it or read it right the first time. Get a second opinion—and if you can, ask the person for clarification.

2. If the person offered it to you verbally, before you respond or assume you understand what the issue is, ask clarification questions based on what you think you heard. Also, try repeating back what you heard to make sure you heard what they were saying clearly first.

3. Avoid offering correction in written form. Never ever do it in an email. (It will be forwarded on, I promise you.) You might have to do a written review because of your work context, but if you can, at least try to avoid giving them a copy. In part, this will keep them from reading it over and over again as if you corrected them 27 times instead of just once. It will also keep them from reading a tone and volume that simply are not there.

4. Whenever possible, after offering a word of correction or a critique, ask the person you're talking with to repeat back what you said. I usually say, "Before we go, can you take a minute and tell me what you heard me say? Let's just assume I'm your friend who in five minutes is going to ask you, 'Hey, what did Brian say to you?' Just to make sure we're clear, can you please tell me what you heard?" Sometimes that simple ending unearths things I need to clear up to avoid a world of downstream problems. Especially in the context of criticism, it is more common than not that something is being miscommunicated.

In terms of my own communication training, I went to college at the University of California at Davis. As a freshman, I was an engineering major. But the summer between my freshman and sophomore years, I felt like God was calling me into youth ministry, so I gathered my own "Quaker Clearness Committee" of sorts to confirm it, and then I changed my major to rhetoric and communication. It seemed logical to me at the time—or at least was the most logical major that a secular school offered and could be applied to my calling. In the process of pursuing my degree, I discovered that every single professor of rhetoric in the world had to write their own model of communication for their Ph.D. If you doubt the depth of this, go ahead and get out your favorite search engine and look up "communication models." Google gave me 60,600,000 image results in .32 seconds.

Some are more famous than others, but all of them have some crazy set of boxes, some method of word flow, and some point of contention where the whole thing can go astray. Aristotle had a very simple one[8]:

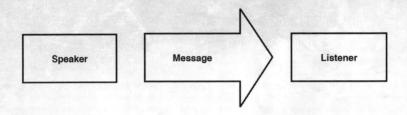

Only problem is, no one believes it's that simple. Have you ever asked a student what he or she heard after your talk? It's scary what people hear. Some people say communication is the biggest barrier between your brain and your mouth. If you're a teacher, you probably believe that's true. Aristotle's model seems to imply that if you reversed the process, the same information would flow the other direction. The assumption is that you're going from your notes, through your speech, and into their notes. But between your notes and their notes, a whole lot of crazy stuff is going on.

William Schramm in the 1950s came up with a model that a lot of people teach. For his model, he changed the names around some. Then he added two big overlapping circles: one labeled *encoding* and one labeled *decoding*. This isn't the exact model, but it's the basic idea with his wording and elements:

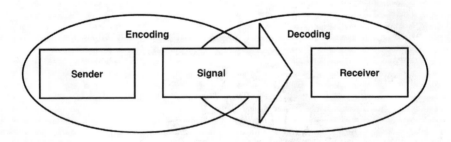

I like this model because it implies that for real clear communication to happen, you need some kind of secret decoder ring. This is more true to my experience. No communication—especially not critical communication—is ever simple or fully heard as it was intended. To get at this truth, some people's communication models attempt to identify the actual source of confusion. They add a box for body language and the various elements that all speakers and listeners bring to an environment. Or they insert squiggly lines for "interference" to show that the whole process is a bit of a mess and that the idea of "you said it, they heard it, and now you both understand the same thing" is ridiculous. In fact, most modern communication models would prove that if we define communication as "a speaker communicating an idea or concept to a listener in such a way that the speaker's idea and the listener's understanding of it are identical," then we'd might as well say communication never happens. There's always interference and confusion.

Have you ever tried to give directions to a student who is blindfolded? It is like you're speaking another language. The other day I told a student to set down a punch bowl on a white table that I pointed to. I looked up and she was still standing there with the bowl, looking confused—and she wasn't even blindfolded. Then my intern said, "Hey Brian, you're gonna have to be more specific. We have white tableclothes on all the tables." Ha! She didn't see where I pointed, and I forgot we had made all the yellow tables white for the event we were setting up for. So stupid and so classic. Seriously, I can't even say, "Put the bowl on the white table" without communication interference and confusion.

For what it's worth, to this end, I made my own communication model for student ministry. Here it is. Good luck.

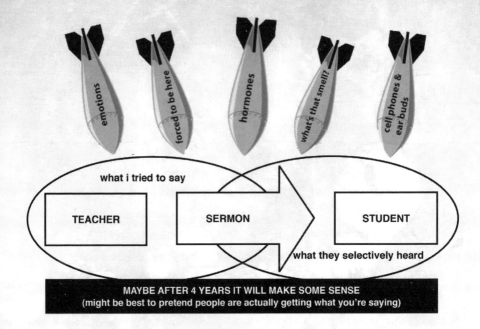

emotions · forced to be here · hormones · what's that smell? · cell phones & ear buds

what i tried to say

TEACHER → SERMON → STUDENT

what they selectively heard

MAYBE AFTER 4 YEARS IT WILL MAKE SOME SENSE
(might be best to pretend people are actually getting what you're saying)

This whole chapter is simply a reminder that when it comes to criticism, there are a thousand opportunities for miscommunication. In fact, you should probably assume it's happening somewhere. Someone is being misread. Something was repeated incorrectly. Some backstory is causing a level of confusion that you and I have no way of being aware of. Communication can be and probably is getting messed up.

However, rather than decide it can't be done and quitting, let me suggest this: Just accept the fact that responding to your critics as well as passing out criticism will require some communication clarification. Live with the assumption that it will require a two-way street and some time. You'll need to ask some good questions, learn to laugh at some misunderstandings, and assume that somewhere along the way, someone is being read incorrectly.

So remember: communication, communication, communication. It is the vehicle in which all of this conflict is happening. Now take some time to clear it up before you declare it a failure and ditch it in the junkyard.

SOME QUESTIONS TO PONDER:

- When was the last time you felt like you were misread or misunderstood? What factors would you identify as common sources of confusion in the communication process?

- Because all criticism involves communication and all communication is complicated, what steps do you need to take to bring about clarity? What patterns or processes do you have in place to help you avoid responding poorly to communication you misread?

- What is your opinion about written correction? Do you agree with what I wrote about it? If you have a different perspective, what is it and why is that your opinion?

- If you were to make your own communication model, what elements would you include in it? What would you add to Aristotle's basic model to make it more complete or accurate?

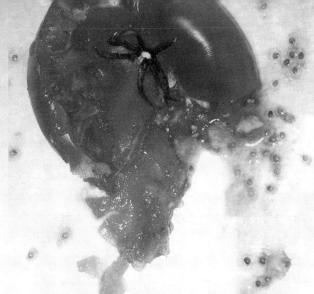

CHAPTER 11
THE BLIND EYE AND THE DEAF EAR

Charles Spurgeon was a famous preacher, pastor, author, visionary, and leader in England who at age 20, in 1854 and long before the days of electronic amplification, was regularly preaching in his church to audiences in excess of 10,000 people. He started an orphanage. He launched a seminary. He wrote prolifically as an author, and many of his works are still in publication today. Many people did and still do call him the "Prince of Preachers." His life and teaching transformed not only England in his day, but the church and the pastorate in the decades ahead. One of the lives he transformed was my own, nearly 100 years after his death when I read an article excerpt from his book called *Lectures to My Students*, in which he wrote a lecture called "The Blind Eye and the Deaf Ear."

When questioned about this principle by his students, he said he discerned it from Ecclesiastes 7:21-22—*Do not pay attention to every word people say, or you may hear your servant cursing you— for you know in your heart that many times you yourself have cursed others.*

We can immediately notice two things in this text. First, not every word people speak is worthy of the same mental attention. Some stuff should clearly be listened to, while some stuff should be ignored. This is especially true when the speaker is your critic. Second, we've all said some things we regret. Who hasn't said something we later wished we could catch in a thought bubble and shove back into the abyss of our gut as if it never was spoken? Perhaps that is why James offered this warning: *But no human being can tame the tongue. It is a restless evil, full of deadly poison. With the tongue we praise our Lord and Father, and with it we curse human beings, who have been made in God's likeness. Out of the same mouth come praise and cursing. My brothers and sisters, this should not be (James 3:8-10).*

But while this should not be the way we use our words, James and Solomon both call out the fact that it is the norm. And far too often, this is the case with criticism, and some of it should be sent back like a bounced check. To this end, we'd be wise to learn to apply a deaf ear and a blind eye to some words and their source, if for no other reason than to give others the grace we desperately need when we speak a word in anger or during some other emotional outburst.

From this text, Spurgeon taught his pupils a variety of situations into which they could apply the principle of a "blind eye and a deaf ear." He argued that from a young age we learn to close our eyes to avoid seeing things we do not wish to see and that wise leaders should learn to develop "ear lids" so as to do the same with things they hear. Spurgeon believed in starting every conversation and every ministry with a blank slate, giving it your good ear and your good eye. But after hearing them out and seeing what our critics are about, sometimes we should turn a blind eye and a deaf ear. Their opinions are not worth the time, and their character is not credible.

As a grid through which I decide who gets the "blind and deaf side" of me and who gets the "seeing and hearing side" of me, I've landed on some key principles worth considering as we wrestle with criticism.

CONSIDER THE SOURCE

If you've done any international traveling and you didn't want to spend all of it sick and puking, then you've learned to ask yourself a few basic questions before eating and drinking, including "What is that?" and "Where did it come from?" The first time I went to Uganda, I spent a lot of time on Lake Victoria visiting mud hut villages with a Christ-follower named Timothy, who was also a church planter. He would take us into these remote villages where the locals would provide us with incredible meals as a way of welcoming us. Honestly, I felt pretty guilty eating it knowing how little food they had and how much we didn't need it. But as we were presented with an array of beans, rice, cabbage, posho, chicken, goat, and fish, we tried to eat a little of everything so as to not be rude.

However, there was one thing I couldn't get up the courage to eat. We affectionately called it "fish eye soup." It was cut-up fish, including the heads, all thrown in a pot and then boiled. The soup would just be sitting in a bowl on the table staring at me, and I'd be asking myself, "Where did that water come from—and is that fish head healthy?" I didn't know enough about the source to verify that it would be safe, so I chose to pass it up every time. However, if it had been presented to us at the guesthouse where we were staying, I might have mustered up the gumption to give it a try. At least there, I knew they had access to good water and I trusted the source to have my fickle American stomach as a concern in preparation.

In a similar way, not all criticism is equal, and we'd be wise to think twice before we digest it. Bill Hybels, senior pastor of one of the largest churches in the United States—Willow Creek Community Church near Chicago—once sent out this tweet: "Criticized as a leader? Expect it. Consider the source. Find the kernel of truth in it. Learn what you can from it. And press on!"[9] I loved it so much that I held on to it and re-read it several times in the coming months. I couldn't agree more. That's some solid advice.

But when it comes to evaluating your source so you can find that nugget of truth and move on, the first question becomes, "How will I know if a source is viable or not?" If my seminary professor were answering the question, he'd be looking for initials after a name and some sort of author credential list. In my case, I'm not looking for graduate-level academic bibliography credentials. I'm looking for character credibility.

I don't have it all figured out, but here are some questions I ask when considering the source.

Is It Anonymous?

After some time and counsel from mentors I trust in the aftermath of various situations, I now try to personally ignore anonymous criticism and counsel others to do the same—not because of what an anonymous note might contain, but what it doesn't contain: a name. If you don't have the guts to sign your own critical letter, then your criticism is not worth my time. I'm not a police department looking for anonymous tips into my soul. If you have something to say to me, then come out and say it, or I'll just trash it.

Part of what allowed me to dismiss that anonymous note I mentioned earlier was what the anonymity said about the source. He (or she) was a rock thrower. That person was not interested in helping me and just wanted to hurt me. That person also was not interested in reconciliation or in being the body of Christ with me, because I cannot do either of those things with a faceless, bitter ghost. As a church staff, we have stopped using comment cards in the pews because far too many were anonymous, and when we can't consider the source, we're forced to give the good eye and the good ear to cynics who have no interest in really helping change anything. So if the source is anonymous, then I consider the source useless, and I'd strongly encourage you to dismiss it altogether.

The only exception to this rule would be if you're willing to give it to several other trusted mentors and friends to read before you give it any credibility. Then ask them, "Would you sign this?" If yes, then seek them for clarity and counsel. If no, then shred it.

How Is the Person's View Impacted by Age and Experience?

In youth ministry, I frequently have to factor in age and experience. This is not to say that I haven't been corrected wisely by a 5-year-old child or that I haven't heard out the criticism and made changes based on the feedback from a 16-year-old young adult. It is just that when I get an opinion from the vantage point that has very little life experience, I need to sit on it longer before I act.

A classic example would be the criticism that we need to do "more events." Some students in my ministry evidently think that we should have the door open 24/7 with a movie or a game night or a worship experience or something. I usually tell them that it's OK to have a life outside the church and that we only have so much any of us can do. When I feel bad and give in to this criticism and decide that we're not doing enough, inevitably I will be the person setting up the event alone, and then the very students that said we needed them won't show up. I've responded to teenagers who cried wolf too many times, and I'm now wiser for it. Not every teenager is the same and not every teenager will get the same response from me, but when evaluating the source, consider that person's age and life experience.

The reverse is also true. I'm careful to give more attention to certain elders and mentors in my life, even if they offer a criticism I disagree with, because they have a vantage point on life I have not yet reached. I cannot simply push them off as too old to "get it." Sometimes they "get" what I simply cannot "get" because I'm 20 (or more) years younger. Peter offers this caution that I try to remember in these situations: *In the same way, you who are younger, submit yourselves to your elders. All of you, clothe yourselves with humility toward one another, because, "God opposes the proud but shows favor to the humble" (1 Peter 5:5)*. Age is not the only factor we ought to consider, but it is one we should not ignore because the experience that comes with it is invaluable for those of us who don't want to learn everything the hard way.

What Is the Person's Attitude Toward Life?
Here's another question worth considering: Is this criticism consistent with past behavior, or is it out of character? Does this person constantly whine about everyone and everything? If so, then you can likely dismiss

the source because you're just the next person in line, and even if you did what this person asked, you're only delaying the next criticism for a little while. That person will be back again to tell you why he or she is right again and why you are wrong, regardless of how you respond this time. If, however, you rarely hear this person complaining, I'd consider giving it a better ear. Something moved this person out of the norm to issue a concern, and it just might be one you need to hear.

Do You Respect This Person's Perspective?

If the source is not actually on your team, then seriously weigh that before giving any credence to the criticism. No, I'm not saying that someone from another department, church, or family can't speak into yours. I'm simply saying that if that person is operating from a different set of basic assumptions about how life should be run, then maybe let that limit the degree to which you give them your good ear.

I once heard a pastor complain that his critics were mad at him for breaking the rules of football when, in his mind, he was playing golf. In other words, if you're not operating under the same basic assumptions about how to do life, then the criticism has less weight. Even Jesus warned his disciples to be leery of giving too much value to the Pharisees and their criticism. *"So you must be careful to do everything they tell you. But do not do what they do, for they do not practice what they preach" (Matthew 23:3).* The Pharisees' words were from the Scriptures, but their lives were not. So Jesus compared them to a tomb that is white on the outside and full of dead bones on the inside. *"In the same way, on the outside you appear to people as righteous but on the inside you are full of hypocrisy and wickedness" (Matthew 23:28).* The Pharisees taught from the same Scriptures, but they were clearly not on the same team as Jesus. They had a very different perspective and were very vocal to Jesus and his disciples about it.

So if I have a friend who is a non-Christian and he is ripping into me for the way I manage my money, I need to consider that our basic premises about how we do or don't spend money are radically different. I'm trying to swim upstream in my consumer culture, and he might be trying to catch a wave. Again, the opposite is true as well. If the word of correction is coming from someone who handles money wisely and I think that there's wisdom in our shared values, then it's worth my time to consider it. The fact that we have the same principles for doing life makes me more willing to give the good eye and the good ear.

As a parent, this comes into play a lot. It's really hard to listen to parenting advice from someone who doesn't parent like I do and has a track record that I don't respect. When they criticize what I'm doing, I tend to give them my deaf ear because we clearly are trying to raise two very different families. If, however, that person has raised a family that I wish I had or has parented in a way that I deeply respect, even if their kids rejected it from time to time, then I might even seek them out and ask for some correction. Perspective matters.

Did This Person Express Criticism in a Healthy Way?

If not all sources should be trusted, then neither should all words be trusted. I have some common "red flag" statements that tell me my source is not fully for me and might have another agenda than my success or the success of my family, my ministry, or whatever else they are criticizing. These "red flag" statements get people nowhere in my world and usually set off alarms in me instead of opening my eyes and ears to give them the attention they want. Maybe you can relate:

They said: "You know, I'm not the only one who feels this way." Here's what I heard: "I've been talking to everyone else before I talk to you—and you know, the majority is usually right." Red flag. Didn't your mom ever ask you, "If a group of kids jumped off a bridge, would you do it?" The majority can easily be wrong. The real issue is why you thought you needed to gather numbers before coming to me with your concern. That's the bigger red flag.

They said: *"You know, so-and-so doesn't do it this way."* Here's what I heard: "I think you should be more like so-and-so because they are the model." Red flag. Who died and made them king? Maybe so-and-so has someone squawking in their ear that they are not like me. Compareanoia (as we talked about in Chapter 4) is a horrible foundation from which to lead.

They said: *"You know, I can take this to your boss."* Here's what I heard: "I like to threaten people and think that this is some kind of power struggle and secret you're hiding." Red flag. This is why I took it to my boss when the problem arose in the first place. Your surprise attack is gone. Wanna go together? I can show you where his office is.

Then there is the flip side. Just as we can ignore some things, we can lean into other things based on words that are spoken. Here's some stuff that tends to turn my good ear in people's direction.

They said: *"I'm sure there's been some kinda misunderstanding, but...."* What I heard: "I'm not here to blame anyone, but I think there's a problem you might want to address." So good. I need people like this in my life.

They said: *"I heard XYZ. Is that true?"* What I heard: "I think this is out of character for you, so before I go believing it, I'm coming to you for clarity." Aces. It is so good to have people in my world that model going to the source for clarity before surfing social media for details. Can I have three more of you?

They said: *"I've been meaning to talk to you about this."* What I heard: "I've been stewing on something for a while now, and I think it's time to talk." Sounds like I should make some time for them.

I hope Spurgeon's blind eye and deaf ear concept has resonated with you. The next time you have a critic bending your ear, before you give them your undivided attention, you can have the confidence to consider the source and evaluate the person and what is being said before you choose to internalize and own it as from God.

But there's one more thing I want to encourage you to do as well.

IDENTIFY SOME DOUBLE-EYE AND DOUBLE-EAR PEOPLE IN YOUR LIFE

No one reading this book thinks they are perfect. (If you did, you wouldn't be reading this kind of book!) None of us believe that we are the one exception to the need for a coach and that we can somehow become all God has made us to be outside of community. None of us think we are above correction or that somehow we've grown so mature that we don't have to improve any longer. In other words, we all realize we will be criticized and can even benefit from it.

So with that in mind, the wise among us will go seeking what I call "double-eye and double-ear" friends and mentors. When these individuals come to me with a concern about my life, I clear my schedule, turn off all distractions, cup my ears, and lean in. I'm giving them full eye contact and listening with the ears of my soul. These are people who consistently pass the source-and-words test. They are on my team. They love God, love me unconditionally, and are not afraid to tell me when I'm getting weird. You won't have 50 of these people, but we all need some of them for sure.

The beauty of people in the double-eye and double-ear crowd is that I never worry when they say, "Hey, I've got some things I want to talk to you about" because I'm confident they always have my best interest in mind. They're not out to rip into me for pleasure. They don't have a bone to pick for fun. They are not disgusted by my weaknesses or enamored by my strengths. They are the kind of people who will tell me that something is funky before my enemies will. They are a gold mine. They are the ones I go to when I need a Quaker Clearness Committee, and often when I just need to get some perspective.

I have a group of pastors and friends that I meet with annually for four days, a mentor I meet with twice a month, and a few friends I go to for counsel. I need their correction, their support, and their insight to become who God has made me to be. They are the ones who will give me an honest and wise response when I say, "Hey, this person said this about me. Does that sound right to you? Have you ever felt this way?"

So my prayer with you and for you is that God will give you the strength to open your eyes and ears to the right people and shut them down to the wrong voices. May the Lord give you discernment as you seek to know when to cup an ear and grab your eyeglasses for some—and the discipline to close your eyes and plug your ears to the damaging voices of others.

SOME QUESTIONS TO PONDER:

- As you consider the source(s) of criticism in your life, what are some factors that cause you to give someone your blind eye or turn your deaf ear toward a person? What are some things that tend to make criticism negatively weigh on you? Would you add anything to the list this chapter gave, or would you highlight any of them as highly relevant to evaluating your critics today?

- What are some factors that tend to give more weight to a word of criticism or correction? When are you most likely to lean in and give others your undivided attention? Who are some of the double-eye and double-ear people you have in your life?

- What are your own views on anonymous criticism? How would you respond to a letter like I received from that anonymous critic?

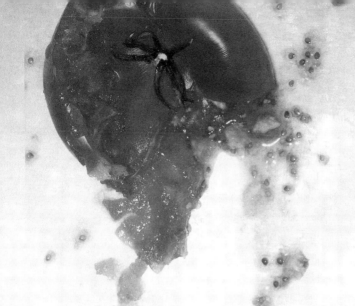

CHAPTER 12
BEFORE YOU DO SOMETHING YOU'RE GOING TO REGRET

When I was in high school I had one goal that I wanted beyond anything else. Surrounding the entire high school gym about 15 feet up from the ground were large wooden shields engraved with the names of athletes who had earned seven varsity letters or more since the founding of our school around 1950. By the late 1980s, they were almost finished with the first row. Because our mascot was the Trojan, it was called the Herculean Award—and plain and simple, I wanted it. Bad. But because we could only play three sports in a year, in order to get it I would have to earn a varsity letter in at least one sport either as a freshman or sophomore.

With this goal in mind, I set my sights on getting my name on the wall. My freshman year I went out for cross country and fainted at the first practice. I didn't have a chance. My sophomore year, I missed varsity in cross country by one place. Then I made it to the last cut in soccer tryouts but played JV instead. Then finally, I only had one shot left: track and field, in the spring. The only way I was going to get a varsity letter as a sophomore was if I won the league meet in my event. That was the only loophole I had. If you got first place at league, they would give you a varsity letter. So I set my sights on that.

I managed to win the two-mile race in our league, and at literally the last possible athletic event of my sophomore year, I reeled in my first varsity letter. Then for the next two years, every day after school you could find me running, playing soccer, or running some more as I racked up my final six varsity letters running cross country, playing soccer, and running long distance in track. And I did it!

Great job, Brian! I know. Impressive, huh? That's what I thought, too, when they handed me my certificate and mounted my name on the wall for generations to come.

That was until one Christmas when I was at my parents' house in my early 20s. After all the presents were unwrapped and people were sitting around enjoying their coffee, my dad walked in with two more surprise gifts: one for my sister and one for me. As I opened up the package and she opened hers, I realized it was my wooden shield. She had achieved the same award two years later, and hers was in her box, too—but in her case, it was split in two.

In shock, with my coveted shield in hand and as my sister held hers in pieces, I looked up at my dad and asked just one question: "Where did you get this?" What he said next was a kick in the gut I never saw coming. He said the school got a new athletic director and they were no longer doing the Herculean Award. "I heard they popped them off and threw them in the Dumpster®, and someone from the school called me to see if I wanted yours," my dad said. "So I dug through to find them."

I didn't know whether to feel overwhelmingly loved by my dad or intensely angry with some unknown director who felt he had he right to destroy an entire high school sports career winnings in one swing of a hammer. Seriously. Who does that? The Dumpster! Really? I felt cheated. I felt betrayed. Countless races and meets and games and practices all flashed across my mind as I realized I had given way too much time, blood, sweat, and tears to become immortalized in my school history, only to discover it didn't even last five years.

If I could go back and do it all over again, I still would have played all those sports (though I might not have worked so hard my sophomore year to win that race), but I definitely would have cut myself some slack. There was way too much on the line for something so temporary. I still can't believe some of those shields were on the wall for almost 40 years, and mine was there for less than five. It took me almost that long to earn it.

And if I could give you one essential piece of criticism advice in this last chapter, it would be this: Be careful that you don't die on a hill that's not worth dying on. Before you go fighting to win…before you stake your ground…before you call out your critic to present some solid evidence… before you blow up that friendship or quit your job or divide your family out of principle, please ask yourself, "Is this something I'm going to regret one day?"

If you don't want the answer to this to be yes, then I have a list of learnings that I want to leave you with as a sort of appendix. It's like a final chapter, in list form, of advice I'd give on the nuts and bolts of responding to your critics. This is the stuff that I've learned from experience, gleaned from friends, and absorbed through reading. I suppose every one of them could have been another chapter, but instead of writing an encyclopedia, I opted for this chapter instead.

So here they are: Before you do or say something you're going to later regret, please…

ASSUME THE BEST IN OTHERS. Start with the basic assumption that your critic is not trying to be mean. They might be defending their kid or protecting their family. Maybe they think they are helping you not hurt someone else or whatever. When they give you a backhanded compliment and say something such as, "For a young pastor, that was pretty good" or "I didn't think this place should have hired you, but I'm really glad they did" or "Wow, for such a big family, your kids were really well-behaved," just assume the second half was what they were trying to say and that the first half was supposed to be encouraging. You can make a dart board with their picture on it later—just do it in your basement and cover it with a poster in case they accidentally wander in there one day.

REMEMBER THAT NO ONE THINKS THEY THREW THE FIRST PUNCH.
You're just going to have to trust me on this one. Every single negative or critical letter you received or conversation you had was defensive on the part of the other person. Seriously. The anonymous note I got was because someone felt attacked by me. The neighbor is mad at you because you don't trim your plants. It was your actions that forced your boss to make this policy that has created conflict. Every. Single. Time. And when you respond to them, you'll think it's in response to their letter. But they won't.

Don't get all scientific on me and tell me that someone has to have started it. The psychological reality doesn't fit the chemistry model. Everyone thinks everyone else started it—and therefore everyone AND no one started it. Get over it. In every conflict, just walk in knowing that no one thinks they threw the first punch. If you're counseling a student and a parent who are at odds with one another, both will say the other one started it. Marriage counseling—same thing. It's no different with you and your critics. So just settle it now, and start every conversation with the basic assumption that the critic you are in a tangle with is under the assumption that they are defending themselves against someone or something. If you want to solve your conflict wisely, figure out what that offense is before you go trying to solve the wrong problem.

ASK GOOD QUESTIONS. The best way to avoid dealing with the wrong conflict is by doing nothing until you've asked a few questions. Ask what they mean by key words or phrases. Tell them what you think you heard them say, and ask them to verify it. Ask them what they think you should do. Ask them what they think the real problem is. Ask them for some time to think about it. In fact, if you're not conniving and are genuine in your questions, you might be able to solve the entire problem without doing anything but asking questions. If you actually manage to pull that off, however, two things must happen. First, you must officially change your middle name to "questionmaster." Second, if you're not one already, become a lawyer. You were made for it.

EXPECT COMMUNICATION PROBLEMS. We already spent a whole chapter on this, so this is just a reminder. Don't make the mistake of believing that because you thought it went really well, that they thought so, too. Work hard to make sure that good communication really is happening, not just assumed to be happening.

GO DIRECTLY TO THE SOURCE AND PUT MATTHEW 18 INTO PRACTICE. Matthew 18:15-17 reads as follows: *"If your brother or sister sins, go and point out their fault, just between the two of you. If they listen to you, you have won them over. But if they will not listen, take one or two others along, so that 'every matter may be established by the testimony of two or three witnesses.' If they still refuse to listen, tell it to the church; and if they refuse to listen even to the church, treat them as you would a pagan or a tax collector."* So if we just follow the textual prompts with this teaching of Jesus, then we will follow a very specific order of events when we confront people because of some sin or error:

1. Go directly to the one you have a conflict with, and try to work it out personally

2. Bring in two or three people who you respect and who are in godly leadership roles

3. Bring it to a larger group of Christ-followers to work it out

4. Boot 'em to the curb, or something like that

While I pray that you never have to get to step 3 or 4, please always start with step 1. Don't go to the person's friends to get clarification first. Don't text your small group or ask 12 people for advice. Just go directly to that person and ask a good question. If you do that, you might actually be on the road toward God-honoring restoration, too.

LISTEN LONG. RESPOND SLOWLY. SPEAK LESS. A phrase found in Psalm 103:8 is repeated nine times in seven different books in the Old Testament: *The Lord is compassionate and gracious, slow to anger, abounding in love.* Go ahead and re-read it at least nine times to get the same emphasis and to drive it deep into your psyche. If you and I are going to respond to our critics in a God-honoring way, then we're going to have to do it at about half-speed. *Slow* seems to be the operable word in that sentence for our culture today. In addition, Proverbs 10:19 says this: *Sin is not ended by multiplying words, but the prudent hold their tongues.* So when it comes to criticism, go ahead and slow it down. Sleep on it. Type your response to that email, but don't send it. Journal. Pray. Most fires will start to die down if you just deprive them of fuel. And then when you do address it, use compassion and grace and love and as few words as possible. God seems to be all about that.

BE THE FIRST ONE TO BRING YOUR BOSS OR SUPERVISOR INTO THE PICTURE. Seriously, this one has saved me on so many occasions. I've taken the wind out of countless sails by being the first one to my boss. I wish I had pictures of people's faces when they went to complain about some event we ran or something I said they didn't like and they said, "Are you aware that Brian…"—only to have the answer be "Yes, he already told me." Don't get me wrong: I don't look for ways to mess up, and I tell my boss the good stuff in my life and ministry, too, but I definitely don't hide the bad stuff. And as a result, my boss is rarely, if ever, surprised with bad news from one of my critics.

On several occasions, it's actually back fired on them and bolstered my confidence when dealing with angry critics. One time, when we taught on homosexuality in our high school ministry, a family was very, very, very angry with me for it. They were not happy with our stance, had gotten some bad information through the "he said, she said" model, and then wrote me a big ol' letter and threatened to leave the church. I showed it to my boss, and he said, "Well, you did the right thing. If they want to leave, then that's their prerogative. Do you want me to go to the meeting with you?" I said, "No, I think I got it" and was able to interact with them in our conference room knowing I had the full support of the lead pastor. That kind of unity saves headaches and is worth way more than any initial conflict I might have created or unearthed by telling it to my boss in the first place.

PRACTICE THE GOLDEN RULE, AND GIVE IT THE SAME WAY YOU WANT TO RECEIVE IT: WITH LOVE, GRACE, AND TRUTH. Luke 6:31 reads, *"Do to others as you would have them do to you."* This should be the opening line of every conflict conversation. When you go to meet with someone who wants to correct you or who you want to correct, you should both raise your right hand and repeat it while gazing in one another's eyes. If we all wrote emails, composed letters, and said words through this filter, we could probably reduce this book to a single sentence and be done.

IF YOU CAN'T SAY IT IN LOVE, DON'T SAY IT. If your critics need to be put in their place or have a thing or two coming from you, then turn around and go back to your office. You're not ready. In 1 Corinthians 13, Paul tells the Corinthian Christ-followers that even if they talk nice, perform miracles, endure criticism, and accomplish great ministry feats but do it without love, then it amounts to nothing. So if your goal in responding to your critics is restoring them, building unity, or helping bring peace, then power on. You have love as your motive. If not, please go back to the drawing board. You're on a path to more criticism and making the problem worse, not better. Oh, and the only thing worse than having to deal with a critic you don't like is having to apologize to that person for your irresponsible words. Be slooooooow to speak, and when you do, do it in love.

SEPARATE PEOPLE FROM THE PROBLEM. Conflict and criticism are like a peanut butter and jelly sandwich: Once you put the two halves together, it's really hard to go back to separate ingredients. If you're having a problem with your spouse about your car, the tendency is to believe that they are the same problem. But they are not. You have a car problem and a relationship problem. When criticism comes, sometimes the best thing you can do is peel the two halves apart and say to the other person, "I really don't think I have an issue with you. What we have is an issue with how we do XYZ." Especially in the church, we ought to be able to separate the issues from the person. We are one through Jesus; we are divided by something else. That's why Paul offers this reminder: *For our struggle is not against flesh and blood, but against the rulers, against the authorities, against the powers of this dark world and against the spiritual forces of evil in the heavenly realms (Ephesians 6:12).* If you can separate the problem from the people attached to it, you'll have a lot less baggage to wade through when it comes to criticism.

DON'T RESPOND IN WRITING. I already pushed this, but I'm going to say it again. This is a bad idea, even if you think you're being gentle. The written word will be read over and over again and it will sound like you've said it 47 times. Your written words will have whatever tone of voice and volume your reader gives it. So if they read it 15 times thinking you're yelling every time, you will have yelled at them 15 times before you two meet face-to-face again—and I guarantee that won't go well. Written stuff gets saved and forwarded and submitted to courts and all kinds of stuff.

Write stuff down for your records or as a guide for your conversation; just don't let it be the main mode of your conflict management. In some situations, such as if I have to fire someone, I'm required to put some things in writing. In that context I do so as a guide and for the "files," and then I personally read it to them in my least favorite meeting in the world to hold. But that's about the only exception. Don't engage in an email thread of criticism. You're going to regret it if you do. Just read the negative comment thread/fight of a blog post, a Facebook page, or a YouTube video to realize that this idea of correcting specific people in writing doesn't work. It always turns out bad.

KILL THEM WITH KINDNESS. When I get to heaven I want to ask Paul about the end of Romans 12. Did he laugh as he wrote it? *Do not take revenge, my dear friends, but leave room for God's wrath, for it is written: "It is mine to avenge; I will repay," says the Lord. On the contrary: "If your enemy is hungry, feed him; if he is thirsty, give him something to drink. In doing this, you will heap burning coals on his head" (Romans 12:19-20).* It's the ultimate kill-them-with-kindness verse. Imagine if it said this: "When people dish out nasty to you, hand them candy back. When you do this, God will make the candy rot their teeth. Amen." Ha! I mean, really—heap burning coals on their head? That's one way to kill them, but it's going to be super painful.

I stole this phrase from my wife because she uses it and it works. Whenever we're somewhere and some employee is giving me the red-tape runaround about how their policy makes it so they can't do something that any sane human being would do, I want to jump across the counter and do it myself. Shannon just says, "Smile and kill them with kindness." So she goes over the top to be nice, acts like she's never caused a problem a day in her life, and then apologizes for making their job so hard. They do backflips and feel bad, too. I just walk away. It's so hard to fight with anyone who won't fight back. So remember the words of Romans 12:18—*If it is possible, as far as it depends on you, live at peace with everyone*—and kill them with kindness. If someone has to get nasty, evidently it should be God alone.

GET A DOG. They love you unconditionally. They'll kiss you and cuddle with you. They don't care what your critics say or how bad your day at the office was. If you take them places, feed them, and go for a walk from time to time, they'll love you forever. If you're lucky, they might even bite your enemy for you. Yup. Get a dog. That's some solid advice right there.

SOME QUESTIONS TO PONDER:

- In this last chapter of advice upon advice, what concept or concepts resonated with you? Why?

- What would you add to this list? What was missing?

- If you ranked the concepts in this chapter as a priority list of sorts, which principles would you list as the top three principles when dealing with critics?

- How has this book shaped you? What ideas or thoughts were new for you? What was a reminder you needed?

- Is there a chapter or a paragraph or even a single sentence that you will hold on to and share with others? If so, what was it—and why?

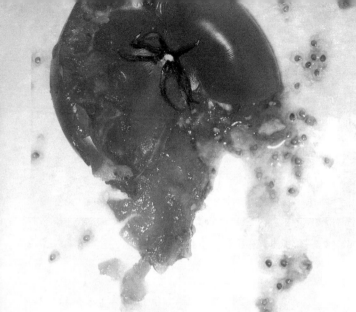

CONCLUSION

A CRITICISM CREED

I hope this book has been an encouragement and a springboard for you in terms of your own process with criticism. My prayer is that it has given you some theological food to think about and some practical ways to implement it into your own life, family, workplace, and church. In the end, I believe criticism is actually a necessary part of all loving relationships. Everyone needs correction from time to time. So as you both receive it and give it, I hope that this book gives you some grace and discernment in the process as you seek to honor God in all you do, especially those emotion-charged and baggage-filled moments when criticism bites.

As a final word, let me propose a creed that we could all stack hands on and agree is the track we'll run on when it comes to criticism. It's an attempt at the collective wisdom of this book in a single page-size creed. Maybe it's even worth posting on your desk or tucking next to your phone for the next time you get one of those calls or emails that have a way of sending you into an emotional and relational tailspin. So how about this—let's agree on these:

- *I will expect criticism to come.*

- *I will seek to please God and love people.*

- *I will invite the Holy Spirit and God-honoring men and women to help me sort through criticism with wisdom and discernment.*

- *I will not harbor resentment, learning to separate discouragement from criticism.*

- *I will learn from my critics, giving appropriate weight according to the source.*

- *I will give criticism how I want to receive it: filled with grace and truth, rooted in love, and offered face-to-face.*

ENDNOTES

1. Live satellite simulcast from the Willow Creek Global Leadership Summit, 2010. Broadcast from South Barrington, Illinois. Viewed in San Diego, California.

2. George Barna, editor, *Leaders on Leadership* (Ventura, CA: Regal Books, 1997), 112.

3. You can find out more about Larry and his ministry at www.b-ing.org.

4. leadership.uoregon.edu/resources/exercises_tips/leadership_reflections/mistakes

5. fgcquaker.org/resources/clearness-committees-what-they-are-and-what-they-do

6. fgcquaker.org/sites/www.fgcquaker.org/files/attachments/Process%20for%20Clearness%20Committees.pdf

7. promisekeepers.org/about/pk-history

8. eou.edu/~rcroft/MM350/CommunicationModels.pdf

9. twitter.com/billhybels (@BillHybels), sent 10/26/11 at 4:08 a.m. The word *kernel* was misspelled as *kernal* in the original tweet, but we chose to correct the spelling in the quoted material.